Coaching for Christian Leaders

The Columbia Partnership Leadership Series
from Chalice Press

www.chalicepress.com
www.thecolumbiapartnership.org

Coaching for Christian Leaders

A Practical Guide

Linda J. Miller
Chad W. Hall

CHALICE
PRESS

ST. LOUIS, MISSOURI

Cover art: FotoSearch
Cover and interior design: Elizabeth Wright

Visit Chalice Press on the World Wide Web at
www.chalicepress.com

10 9 8 7 6 5 4 3 2   07 08 09 10 11 12

Library of Congress Cataloging–in–Publication Data

Miller, Linda J., 1949-
Coaching for Christian leaders : a practical guide / by Linda J. Miller and Chad W. Hall.
  p. cm.
  ISBN 978-0-8272-0507-9
1. Christian leadership. 2. Personal coaching. 3. Church work. I. Hall, Chad W. II. Title.
BV652.1.M543 2007
253–dc22

2007015289

Printed in the United States of America

This book is dedicated to

My closest companions in this journey of life: my family. My dad and mom, Claude and Judy Hall, provided the support I needed to become a lover of learning and a pursuer of dreams. Thank you for displaying appropriate portions of mercy and strength in my life. My daughter, Sydney, inspires me with her intelligence and determination. My sons, Davis and Dean, remind me that life is full of fun, if you just know where to look. Finally, my wife, Holly, is the best person I know–by far. I thank God that He gave her a double portion of patience that has allowed her to endure my wild pursuits, including the fanatical notion of writing a book. She continues to believe in me, encourage me, and stay up late at night dreaming dreams with me. Without her love and support, I would not have written this book.

Chad

My best friend and the love of my life (other than Jesus Christ), my husband Don. You have always believed in me, stretched me in my own beliefs, and encouraged me, even when neither of us knew what would be ahead. I consider you to be a gift from God. I love you.

My daughters, Niki and Krista. It has been a privilege and a blessing to watch you grow into beautiful young women. My prayer for you has always been and will always be the words of verse 4 in 3 John: "I have no greater joy than to hear that my children are walking in the truth."

Several special friends who are also family: My mother and brother, who teach me so much, and Terri, who has become such a good friend. What a testament to the truth that new life comes out of death. You have given me a fresh perspective on life.

Linda

Contents

Editor's Foreword

Inspiration and Wisdom for Twenty-First-Century Christian Leaders

You have chosen wisely in deciding to study and learn from a book published in **The Columbia Partnership Leadership Series** with Chalice Press. We publish for

- Congregational leaders who desire to serve with greater faithfulness, effectiveness, and innovation.
- Christian ministers who seek to pursue and sustain excellence in ministry service.
- Members of congregations who desire to reach their full kingdom potential.
- Christian leaders who desire to use a coach approach in their ministry.
- Denominational and parachurch leaders who want to come alongside affiliated congregations in a servant leadership role.
- Consultants and coaches who desire to increase their learning concerning the congregations and Christian leaders they serve.

The Columbia Partnership Leadership Series is an inspiration- and wisdom-sharing vehicle of The Columbia Partnership, a community of Christian leaders who are seeking to transform the capacity of the North American Protestant church to pursue and sustain vital Christ-centered ministry. You can connect with us at www.TheColumbiaPartnership.org.

Primarily serving congregations, denominations, educational institutions, leadership development programs, and parachurch organizations, the Partnership also seeks to connect with individuals, businesses, and other organizations seeking a Christ-centered spiritual focus.

We welcome your comments on these books, and we welcome your suggestions for new subject areas and authors we ought to consider.

George W. Bullard Jr., Senior Editor
GBullard@TheColumbiaPartnership.org

The Columbia Partnership,
905 Hwy 321 NW, Suite 331, Hickory, NC 28601
Voice: 866.966.4TCP, www.TheColumbiaPartnership.org

Acknowledgments

Life really is a journey. The leg of our journey culminating in publication of this book has involved many dear friends, prized mentors, and wonderful supporters. Allow us to invest a few paragraphs giving credit where it is so deserved.

Ultimate credit goes to the Subject of much of this book: the God who has revealed Himself in Jesus Christ and continues to bless the world through the working of His Holy Spirit. Our prayer is that this book contributes to the Lord's will that things on earth will resemble things in heaven.

To those pioneers who introduced me to the world of coaching, I am forever grateful. Jane Creswell, George Bullard, and Don Bouldin demonstrated vision and generosity in offering training, mentoring, and that most cherished of gifts: opportunity. I would not be a coach if not for them.

My coaching colleagues at Valwood Christian Leadership Coaching and the Baptist State Convention of North Carolina gave me room to discover, develop, and deliver new insights in coaching. They also granted me the key to growth: permission to mess up. Colleagues such as Eddie Hammett, David Moore, John Jones, and Rick Hughes have been colearners and partners in exploring how coaching can serve the world of ministry. Along with Kim Duncan, they have been willing to adjust training schedules, tweak workshop agendas, and scrap PowerPoint presentations to experiment with my latest venture in seeing if a new idea would fly or flop.

Chad

To my Blanchard colleagues and friends—what a fabulous experience it has been to work with all of you! Thanks to Madeleine Homan, my thought partner who pushes me to continue growing, and to Joni Wickline, Patricia Overland, Mary Ellen Sailer, and Adam Morris, all of whom I consider good friends as well as partners inside Blanchard. And, hats off to Scott Blanchard who had the vision of bringing coaching into The Ken Blanchard Companies!

Special thanks to my dear friend and partner in creating and launching the coaching curriculum at Western Seminary, Jane Creswell, and to the leaders and students who have worked hard with us in the past years. I so appreciate Dr. Norm Thiesen, director and professor of record for the coaching program; Steve Thomas, director of enrollment management;

and Dr. Bert Downs, president at Western Seminary, who saw the possibilities for coaching and had the courage to step out in faith. What a blessing it has been to partner with you to launch coaching in a seminary setting.

Linda

A very special thanks to our writing companion, Margaret "Grit" Dempsey. Margaret has become a good friend as she adeptly navigated us through this project, serving us as editor, organizer, translator, and encourager. In so many ways, she "coached" us through the process of writing this book, a new endeavor for both of us. Her intelligence, insight, diligence, redirection (when needed!), and humor have served us well. Margaret, you have been a precious gift from God.

We also want to thank Amy Weeda, who did research for us, or anything else that we asked. Thank you for your quick responses, commitment to us, firm foundation in the Lord, and attention to details.

To our ministry partners at The Columbia Partnership who are visionaries and who are willing to see the power and effectiveness of coaching, thank you for challenging us to keep expanding and seeking the Lord in our ministries. Thank you for believing in us to represent coaching well.

And thanks to the inspirational pastors who have participated in the Sustaining Pastoral Excellence (SPE) grant. You have been a blessing to each of us as we have walked beside you. May you experience God's presence as you serve Him daily.

And, finally, to the hundreds of persons who have allowed us to train and/or coach them. You have taught us so much about how coaching can serve Christ by supporting those who serve in His name. Every workshop, seminar, class, and coaching session has been research for this book. The women and men who trust us enough to call us "coach" are the biggest contributors to this book. The narratives, examples, and many of the insights in this book come from our wonderful clients, who prove every day that people are created in the image of God and have the potential to do great things through Christ. Confidentiality prevents us from listing each of the special clients who have contributed to this book, but each is listed in our hearts and minds. Thank you.

Chad and Linda

Introduction

Life is a story of improvement. The holy Christian writings attest that a central theme of existence is the movement toward better. Genesis starts with God's initial improvement project of order over chaos, with each day unfolding a new and better aspect of God's creation. Revelation and other texts refer to an "end" that is really a new and better beginning. Between genesis and ultimate renewal, each Christ-follower is striving to live a story of improvement—always moving toward fuller connection with God, better community with others, clearer expression of vocation, healthier habits of the heart, more effective use of time, and even improved performance of hobbies and leisure activities.

The believer's God-ordained improvement story doesn't always go that well. An individual gets lazy, runs up against obstacles, or sometimes becomes confused about which way to go and what to do. To reach full potential, a believer might need some help.

This book aims at equipping you to play a supporting role in the lives of others—supporting their (and your) improvement through the practice of Christian coaching.

The Context for Coaching

Today's world calls for a coaching approach for supporting others as they move forward, be it in ministry or in any other setting. The days of static and predictable circumstances are waning. Dee Hock, founder of VISA International and author of *Birth of the Chaordic Age,* said, "Change has changed."[1] The compression of time and events is creating a world in

---

[1]Dee Hock, telephone conversation, May 22, 2000. Also see "An Interview with Dee Hock," http://www.coolchurches.com/articles/deehock.html (May 15, 2006) and Dee Hock, *Birth of the Chaordic Age* (San Francisco: Berrett–Koehler Publishers, 1999).

which things change, not only at a faster rate, but also in directions and dimensions that defy predictability or pattern. The answer to, "What's next?" is no longer evident by examining past successes. In such a context, Christian coaching is an appropriate response because it enables one to relate to others not as an expert who knows the way from experience but as a partner who can help discover the way.

Founder of VISA on Today's Context

People think of this as movement from the industrial age to the information age. The industrial age was really the age of machine-crafting, which is primarily an extension of muscle. Information is the raw material of the mind, which means that it's really the age of mind-crafting. You can also tie that to an amazing transformation— a complete switch in less than fifty years from a time when the value of the physical content of all goods and services was more than 90 percent to a time when the value of the mental content of all goods and services will be more than 90 percent. We're experiencing radically different, ever changing societal diversity and complexity and trying to manage it with archaic, seventeenth-century concepts of organization and management. It demands extraordinarily different concepts of organizations, management, and societal structures.[2]

Discovering the way is vital for today's churches and leaders. Anyone God is using to help spread the reign of Christ can use coaching. This book is designed to bring the positive benefits of coaching more fully to bear on the work of Christ in today's world.

Coaching

Coaching is a growing discipline that has gained much traction in recent years. A simple online search will return hundreds of books, Web sites, and other resources on coaching. This unique approach to helping has become a profession that goes far beyond its sometimes simple expression in athletic coaching. As an art and science of supporting people's forward movements, coaching is impacting families, Fortune 500 companies, ministries, organizations, schools, and government agencies.

Coaching is a fast-growing profession. The International Coach Federation (ICF) membership had reached 10,000 by early 2006, and a large percentage of coaches do not belong to ICF. Coaches work within organizations as diverse as IBM, Capital One, and Northpoint Community Church outside of Atlanta. Others have launched their own coaching practices, allowing them to work with diverse clienteles. No matter the setting, context, topic, or persons involved, coaching is a way to help others

---

[2]From "An Interview with Dee Hock."

improve. The astounding growth of the profession attests to its power and increasing impact. Coaching is growing because it works.

Like other growing professions in the past, coaching is moving into a stage of higher expectations, continued quality improvement, and tighter standards of what it means to be a coach. While the ICF (www.coachfeder-ation.org) has become the most recognized credentialing agency for the profession, a growing constellation of training organizations is emerging to provide quality training for those entering the profession. Many professionals are even using coaching within noncoaching roles. Managers, leaders, counselors, pastors, salespersons, teachers, and others are finding the skills of coaching to be useful complements to their primary roles.

One exciting area of growth in coaching is within Christian ministry. Christ-followers have found coaching to be a natural fit for relationally supporting others to live lives of improvement. Christian coaches are rising to the top of the field: holding important positions within the ICF, setting the standard for results-producing coaching, and making a positive impact though coaching in both church and non-ecclesial settings.

This Book

Excellent books on coaching abound. Experienced authors have produced well-written and thought-provoking works to move readers forward in their coaching. In comparison, relatively few have focused on coaching from a Christian perspective, and even fewer have taught readers how to coach from a thoroughly Christian theological perspective. This book aims at helping you learn how to coach as a part of Christ's activity in the world and as a part of your ministry. As coaching has continued to grow and find increasing expression among Christians, the need has become evident for a user-friendly book that not only introduces people to coaching, but also equips readers with a foundational skill set and approach to coaching. This book is written for readers who want a first-class introduction to coaching and who seek a Christian coaching perspective. Pastors, students, lay leaders, denominational workers, parish staff, and ministers of all types will find this book useful and encouraging.

Loyalties

Readers should find two deep loyalties in these pages. The first deep loyalty is the one this book holds to the historic, timeless truths of Christianity. We do not propose a novel set of beliefs. We do not offer a new interpretation of the Christian faith. We do not skirt the deep truths of Christianity, and we do not give mere lip service to Christian teachings. Rather, this book is solidly grounded in the claims Christ and His followers made. This book is intended to be an expression of Christ's kingdom on earth.

Coaching squares with orthodox Christian theology and provides a powerful expression of Christian faith—one that impacts the world for kingdom good. Coaching is a real-life means of living out the Christian faith according to six core Christian beliefs.

1. *Meaning.* Acknowledging that the here and now holds meaning, Christian coaching brings a redemptive power to the present. Coaching affirms life as a moving, memorable, and meaningful story and seeks to help individual believers align the stories of their lives with the narratives toward which God is directing them.

2. *Potential.* Coaching affirms that God has created each person with enormous general and specific potential that is intended to be released. Coaches care genuinely and work tirelessly to germinate and grow the potential of those they coach. Christian coaches invest relational energy in helping people discern and live into their God-given potential.

3. *Sanctification.* Coaches are in the "sanctification" business. Believers are on a journey toward "saintliness"—not a state of holiness that removes people from the everyday and mundane, but a commitment to walking through life according to the will and ways of Jesus. Coaches help people move forward, exploring challenges and opportunities of life and shifting behaviors and attitudes toward heaven.

4. *Action.* Christians believe the material world is the dwelling place of the spiritual. Coaching encourages people to reflect on what is true and to act in new ways based on this reflective encounter with truth. Christian coaches want people to take intentional action determined from thoughtful consideration of reality, possibilities, barriers, opportunities, and outcomes. The coaching relationship creates space for a person being coached to slow down, become focused, and think through the personal journey of life.

5. *Stewardship.* Coaching supports the Christian belief of stewardship by giving positive attention to the results of a life lived with intention. A part of God's intention is that each individual bear fruit. Coaching invests attention in exploring the results a person is getting, the level of satisfaction with the results, and how poor results can be a doorway into investigating habits, attitudes, beliefs, and actions that produce the results.

6. *Relationships.* The relational nature of coaching reflects the heart of the Christian faith. Coaching is a relationship that fertilizes, nurtures, and even sometimes prunes so that people can live well and bear fruit. A coach is similar to the biblical term *paraclete,* one who comes alongside to assist. Christ used this term to describe the Holy Spirit, who would be a Helper for God's people as they moved through and toward life. The coaching relationship encourages coaches to be used by God in the *paraclete* role for others.

The second deep loyalty that this book holds is a passion for excellent coaching. Christian coaching is not "coaching lite." Christians should be, not only good coaches but also standard-bearers for the coaching profession. Christians have a unique and powerful foundation for this way of helping. Since coaching is about supporting people as they improve, Christian coaches should strive to be the best-in-the-world at this endeavor because doing so is a part of Christians' holy calling and giftedness. These loyalties to Christianity and to coaching are not held in tension, but in unison.

Eleven Core Competencies of a Coach

A. Setting the Foundation
   1. Meeting Ethical Guidelines and Professional Standards
   2. Establishing the Coaching Agreement
B. Co-Creating the Relationship
   3. Establishing Trust and Intimacy with the Client
   4. Coaching Presence
C. Communicating Effectively
   5. Active Listening
   6. Powerful Questioning
   7. Direct Communication
D. Facilitating Learning and Results
   8. Creating Awareness
   9. Designing Actions
   10. Planning and Goal Setting
   11. Managing Progress and Accountability

From International Coach Federation, www.coachfederation.org

Organization of the Book

The organization and specific chapters of this book are designed to give believers the basic tools to begin their endeavors in coaching. This book serves as a starting point for those who are exploring how God can use the discipline of coaching uniquely and effectively in personal ministry. A serious commitment to continuing development as Christian coaches is encouraged.

This book is organized around five general ways of moving you forward in your understanding and practice of Christian coaching:

1. Insights from the authors set the pace and direction for the learning. These insights will convey truth, form the conversation, and tie together the truths offered by others.
2. Narratives add color and context to the learning. These real-life examples and expressions of coaching give more than just a glimpse of what real coaching looks like. The names and details of these narratives

have been changed to protect confidentiality, but the basic story lines and lessons have not been changed.

3. The text is seeded with a variety of visual learning tools, such as sidebars, graphs, charts, bullets, and so on to facilitate, clarify, and highlight the learning.

4. At each chapter's conclusion, a prayer is offered to focus the truths of a particular chapter with their grounding in the truths of Christ.

5. Also at each chapter's conclusion are a series of coaching questions and challenges to help the reader practice what has been taught in the chapter. These "beyond the book" exercises are designed to maximize the learning experience of this book by getting the reader to practice coaching while reading the book.

Overview of Chapters

The book begins with an overview of the world of coaching in chapter 1. With the growth of the coaching profession has come many competing notions of what coaching is, what a coach does, and what one should expect from coaching. This chapter will help the reader "unlearn" some coaching misconceptions, while also providing a helpful overview of the coaching profession. The overview will highlight a brief history of coaching, an introduction to the ICF, basic coaching principles, parameters for when to coach and when to help in a different way, key players in the Christian coaching field, and how coaching is currently being used.

Chapters 2 and 3 are concerned with the skills of coaching. They offer the basic "how to" aspects for learning to coach. Many of these skills will be familiar practices. These chapters help the reader rearrange the familiar skills alongside some new or underdeveloped skills to build a skill set that forms the foundation for great coaching.

Chapter 4 provides models for applying the coaching skills. Rather than rely on one model, this chapter introduces several effective models, each of which uses the skills covered in chapters 2 and 3, giving form and guidance to their application.

Chapter 5 discusses the practical issues of how to establish and conclude the coaching relationship. This chapter covers the nuts and bolts of how to talk with a potential client, how to establish a coaching covenant, and how to begin well and serve each coaching client. The chapter ends with how the coaching relationship reaches a healthy conclusion.

Chapters 6 and 7 explore how coaching can be used, with insight into how coaching fits in the context of Christian ministry. Chapter 6 places coaching alongside other Christian leadership skills, helping paint the distinct nature of coaching in comparison, contrast, and companionship to the other ways of leading. Chapter 7 describes how coaching can positively impact various ministries of a congregation. Finally, several appendices will help the reader take real steps toward expressing quality coaching.

Getting the Most from This Book

This book is designed to be read and referenced, engaged and re-engaged. The reader who wants to move forward and deeper in a personal journey as a Christian coach might consider making three passes through the text.

Begin with a quick introductory sweep through the book to understand the book's scope and how the parts of the book fit together. Next, take a deliberate pass, investing time with each chapter and giving intentional attention to the prayer and assignments at each chapter's end. Carry out the assignments rather than moving too quickly to the next chapter. Put new knowledge into action. Finally, soon after reading all the chapters, skim back through the book to lock in the holistic learning.

Beyond reading the book, keep it handy as a reference book during the first years of putting coaching into practice. Coaching challenges and opportunities will highlight how the book connects with real-life experiences. The book and the experiences should complement one another and make all of coaching clearer.

Also, consider reading the book with a friend or as a part of a book club, class, or small group. While this book is designed for classroom use, everyday readers should find much to discuss with friends and fellow students of life. The exercises at each chapter's conclusion should help facilitate discussion and exploration of concepts in community.

Finally, engage the book by teaching others how to coach. "Third-person teaching" is one of the best ways to take learning to the next level. If a lesson or principle is particularly helpful, find an audience (family, colleague, friend) who can also benefit from the truth and share it!

A Prayer for Beginning

God, thank You for that which is new. As readers embark on the journey of reading this book, we thank You for the curiosity that drew them to begin, the momentum that will move them through the book, and the commitment that will sustain them to turn each page.

Thank You that You are the God of beginnings—creating and always recreating us into Your holy image. May this book be Your handiwork for doing a new thing in each reader as we grow into the likeness of Christ, our Lord. Amen.

Beyond the Book

1. As you begin this book, what are your expectations?
2. What has piqued your interest so far? What three or four themes might you want to be on the lookout for as you read?
3. What new learning have you already picked up? Whom can you share this with and for what impact?

1

Overview of Coaching

▦ ▦ ▦ As soon as Lee arrived at the church, he remembered that he had his first coaching call with Terry that morning. Terry had asked him to be prepared to talk about things that would make a difference for him. As the leader for the church's small group ministry, Lee was pleased with how many groups were flourishing; yet he knew that several were not.

Right on time, Lee's phone rang. After greeting each other, Terry asked Lee where he wanted to focus, and Lee began sharing about several of the small groups that seemed to be struggling. When Terry asked, "What else can you do to help those groups?" Lee realized that he hadn't been spending as much time with those leaders as the others.

Terry continued, "The leaders with whom you've invested time are flourishing in their small groups. How can the leaders of the other groups get what they need?" Like a bolt of lightning, Lee recognized that he might be standing in the way of the leaders' success.

"I need to reach out to them just like I reached out to the others. It didn't take much time, and I can see the fruits of the time spent with each one."

Terry anchored the action by asking, "By when will you meet with each one, Lee?" Lee was ready to make the calls and set up the meetings. ▦

What is coaching? Such a simple question opens the floodgates into a new and rapidly emerging field. If you were to ask twenty people how they would define coaching, you would get twenty different answers. Everyone defines coaching differently. This chapter is intended to look at some of the individual pieces of the "coaching" puzzle and to explore both a definition of Christian coaching and a brief historical development of the discipline.

The Definition of Coaching

The Original Definition

A hundred years ago, a coach was a transport vehicle, as commonly remembered in the story of Cinderella. Riding in a coach meant that a person would be moved from one point to another. In *Webster's Dictionary* the first definition of *coach* is, "a large, covered, four-wheeled carriage used as a conveyance, with seats for passengers inside and an open raised seat in front for the driver: stagecoach."[1]

Today, coaching is similar. Coaching is still about forward movement and action. A coach, however, is no longer a physical vehicle like a car. A coach is a person who facilitates actions that transport people from one place to another, from where they are to a new destination. Until recently, most people connected coaching with the athletic arena. Often after the statement, "I am a coach," the natural response is, "Really? What sport?"

Coaching, as it is used within this book, is not about sports or "winning." It's about taking intentional action, moving forward, and improving performance. By nature, coaches desire to help people improve, change, recognize and use their strengths and talents, and be successful. Christian coaches want all this as well as to know that God's leadership and will are central in the coaching process.

Modern Definitions

Gary Collins, an early adopter within the Christian counseling and Christian coaching arenas, defined coaching as an "art and practice of guiding a person or group from where they are toward the greater competence and fulfillment that they desire."[2]

In one of the first coaching books, Sir John Whitmore proposed, "Coaching is as much about the way things are done as what is done. Coaching delivers results in large measure because of the supportive relationship between the coach and the coachee, and the means and style of the communication used. The coachee does acquire the facts, not from the coach but from within himself, stimulated by the coach."[3]

According to Dennis Kinlaw, "Successful coaching is a mutual conversation that follows a predictable process and leads to superior performance,

---

[1]Victoria Neufeldt, ed. in chief, *Webster's New World Dictionary* (New York: Prentice Hall, 1994), 266.
[2]Gary Collins, *Christian Coaching* (Colorado Springs: NavPress, 2001), 16.
[3]John Whitmore, *Coaching for Performance* (London: Nicholas Brealey, 1995), 4.

commitment to sustained improvement, and positive relationships."[4]

Thomas Crane defined coaching as

> a comprehensive communication process in which the coach provides performance feedback to the coachee. Topics include broad, work-related dimensions of performance (personal, interpersonal, or technical) that affect the coachee's ability and willingness to contribute to meaningful personal and organizational goals...Coaches help people clarify and reconnect to their purposes, values and roles. A coach acts as a guide by challenging and supporting people in achieving their performance objectives.[5]

The ICF, the largest professional association that oversees the coaching profession (outside of athletics), certifies coaches and accredits training programs. According to the ICF Web site, "Personal and business coaching is an ongoing professional relationship that helps people produce extraordinary results in their lives, careers, businesses or organizations."[6]

Definition from a Christian Perspective

From a Christian perspective, coaching is a relationship that involves Christ's presence and truths from Scripture along with high standards as a coach. This equation might be viewed like a mathematical formula:

Christ's vision and mission

+ Scriptural principles
+ Christ's presence
+ High standard of excellence as a trained coach

= Christian Coaching [7]

With such a wide-ranging variety of coaching definitions, individuals can become easily sidetracked in examining and comparing the varying nuances of each definition. Therefore, to help target focus and direction, one overarching definition of Christian coaching will be the cornerstone of this book, a definition that positions the coaching relationship as the cornerstone of coaching, just as Jesus Christ is the cornerstone of the church and our relationship with God.

Christian coaching is a focused Christ-centered relationship that cultivates a person's sustained growth and action.

To help envision the coaching relationship, examine Figure 2.1. Let's unpack some of the meaning conveyed in this illustration.

[4]Dennis Kinlaw, *Coaching for Commitment* (San Francisco: Jossey Bass/Pfeiffer, 1999), 30.
[5]Thomas Crane, *The Heart of Coaching* (San Diego: FTA Press, 1998), 30–31.
[6]ICF, www.coachfederation.org.
[7]Jane Creswell, Western Seminary coaching course MCS 501, 2005.

The Christian Coaching Relationship

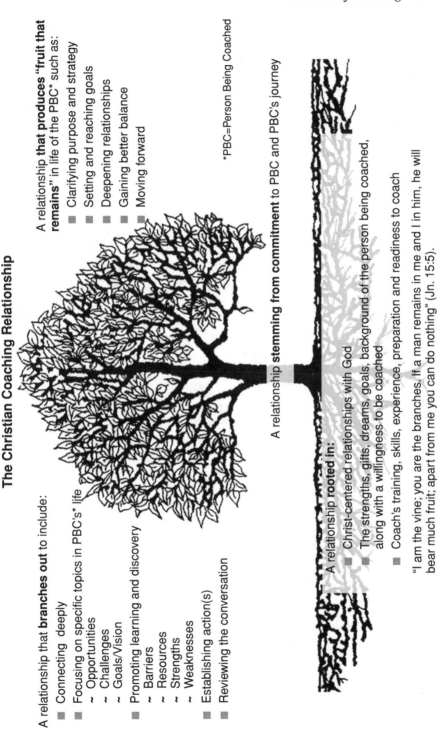

A relationship that **branches out** to include:

- Connecting deeply
- Focusing on specific topics in PBC's* life
  - ~ Opportunities
  - ~ Challenges
  - ~ Goals/Vision
- Promoting learning and discovery
  - ~ Barriers
  - ~ Resources
  - ~ Strengths
  - ~ Weaknesses
- Establishing action(s)
- Reviewing the conversation

A relationship **that produces "fruit that remains"** in life of the PBC* such as:

- Clarifying purpose and strategy
- Setting and reaching goals
- Deepening relationships
- Gaining better balance
- Moving forward

*PBC=Person Being Coached

A relationship **stemming from commitment** to PBC and PBC's journey

A relationship **rooted in:**

- Christ-centered relationships with God
- The strengths, gifts, dreams, goals, background of the person being coached, along with a willingness to be coached
- Coach's training, skills, experience, preparation and readiness to coach

"I am the vine; you are the branches. If a man remains in me and I in him, he will bear much fruit; apart from me you can do nothing" (Jn. 15:5).

"A focused Christ-centered relationship..."

Focused: Christian coaching is purposeful in intent. It is not a relationship for the sake of relationship. It is a relationship with a precise and stated reason for being. The focus in a coaching relationship is always on the person being coached and supporting that person's growth and action.

Christ-centered: The primary distinction that sets Christian coaching apart from all other coaching is its Christ-centeredness. Apart from Christ, there is no Christian coaching. The assumption in Christian coaching is that the coach is a Christian. The person being coached may or may not be a believer. The coach's faith impacts the entire coaching relationship, including attitudes toward the person being coached and the situation being discussed, use of skills in the coaching conversation, perspectives, as well as holy nudges from the Holy Spirit.

Relationship: Coaching, in its essence, is relational. For the Christian coach, the relationship includes the coach, person being coached, and Christ. Because of the unique strengths, gifts, dreams, goals, and backgrounds of the person being coached along with the unique training, skills, experience, and preparation of the coach, each coaching relationship is unique. It is a relationship with a commitment. The commitment is to Christ and to the person being coached.

"...that cultivates a person's sustained growth and action."

Cultivates: Cultivation occurs in conversation. Coaching conversations are the necessary sunshine and water to cultivate the coaching relationship. Through coaching conversations, with the coach using the eight skills outlined and discussed later in this book, the person being coached is able to focus on specific personal opportunities or challenges, anticipate barriers, identify resources, and develop an action plan.

A person's sustained growth and action: Coaching is about transformation. Coaching without sustained growth and action on the part of the person being coached is not true coaching. Christian coaching always, without exception, results in action. The coach supports the person being coached in developing action plans as well as systems of accountability for following through on those plans.

Roots, Branches, and Fruit of the Coaching Relationship

Now, consider the roots, branches, and fruit of the coaching relationship.

Roots–Preparedness

"So then, just as you received Christ Jesus as Lord, continue to live in him, rooted and built up in him, strengthened in the faith as you were taught, and overflowing with thankfulness" (Col. 2:6–7).

These words of instruction from Paul to the Colossian believers are vital for the Christian coach, as well as for the person being coached, if that person is a believer. Quite often, deepening roots with God allow for deepening exploration, discovery, and action in the coaching relationship.

Choosing to be coached makes a powerful statement about an individual's readiness to move forward in life, ministry, or work relationships, or in a myriad of other arenas. For coaching to be successful, the person being coached needs to be ready and willing to engage in a coaching relationship. Starting with the first conversation and throughout the coaching journey, the focus will remain on the strengths, goals, areas for development, and specific situations of the person being coached. As different areas are addressed, the willingness of the person being coached to explore and to take action is critical to the coaching process.

Preparedness by the coach is also important. Each coach brings to the coaching relationship a different level of training, skills, and experiences. The wise coach is well prepared for each coaching conversation so that full attention can be given to the person being coached. Being prepared means being able to focus on and be fully present with the person being coached, being in a place without interruptions, and being ready to concentrate on whatever the person being coached brings to the conversation. Commitment to the Lord, to the coaching relationship, and to the journey of the person being coached is paramount to strong coaching.

The Christian coach's personal commitment to God provides roots and stability for the coaching relationship. The coach's relationship with God positively impacts the coach's relationship with the person being coached. In all aspects of the ongoing coaching relationship, the coach should seek God's wisdom and discernment as the person being coached moves forward.

Branches–The Coaching Relationship through Coaching Conversations

At the core of Christian coaching are relationships–first with Christ, then with others. The model for this centrality of relationships is found in Jesus' greatest commandment, "'Love the Lord your God with all you heart and with all your soul and with all your mind.' This is the first and greatest commandment. And the second is like it: 'Love your neighbor as yourself'" (Mt. 22:37–38). The coaching journey unfolds as the connection between coach and the person being coached is established. In Christ, deep connections support all interactions. Throughout the coaching experience, the focus remains on the topics that the person being coached brings to each conversation. This includes challenges, opportunities, goals, objectives, or specific circumstances.

Throughout coaching, the coach encourages the person being coached to learn and discover new things about God, life, relationships, impact of behaviors, and self. Interestingly, because coaches are always seeking to improve their skills and knowledge and because coaching is a collaborative experience, often both the coach and the person being coached learn and grow. The growth of the person being coached comes as a result of taking action, and the coach grows through participation in the journey of the person being coached.

Coaching is about taking intentional action aligned with God's will and with the desired outcomes of the person being coached. Establishing specific actions is a critical part of coaching and occurs during each coaching conversation. Sometimes, only one or two actions are identified; at other times, the person being coached develops a thorough action plan. Either way, a brief review of actions concludes the coaching conversation.

The Christian life is a life of both reflection and action. One without the other creates an imbalance. Christian coaching affirms learning and discovery in the life of the person being coached, not for the sake of learning and discovery in and of themselves, but, rather, for the sake of establishing appropriate and God-honoring action.

Fruit–Bringing out the Best

As the coaching relationship progresses, fruit develops. Fruit can be internal or external. Internal fruit includes a deeper walk with God, clarity of vision and values, or simply a better quality of life. External fruit includes reached goals, changed relationships, or increased effectiveness within ministry. Just like a bowl with a variety of fruits, coaching brings out the best in people as they grow, change, and deepen their walks with the Lord.

Christian coach Eddie Hammett has said that coaching has borne more fruit, quicker, and with greater effectiveness than any other ministry in which he has been involved. In workshops in which he has shared this statement, he has often received pushback from participants. The uneasiness usually revolves around giving attention to results. As one participant said, "Jesus is much more concerned about our hearts and our intentions than with our results." The origins of such protests are understandable. Christians, churches, and ministries that are too focused on "the bottom line" can mistake peripheral issues for the main thing. Sometimes measurable results can overtake simple obedience to Christ.

However, the New Testament *does* show that Jesus was interested in the results of ministry efforts. In the parable of the talents (Mt. 25:14–30), Jesus told the story of three servants who received varying levels of responsibility and were held accountable for the results of their investing strategies. In another account, Jesus cursed a fig tree that had stopped producing fruit (Mt. 21:18–19). As these and other passages testify, God expects fruit.

This idea of bearing fruit is often referred to as stewardship. Coaching supports Christian stewardship by giving positive attention to the results of a life lived with intention. Coaching conversations often begin by acknowledging that bad or little fruit is being produced. People are not satisfied with the results they are getting and want to get better results. Coaching invests attention in exploring the results a person is getting, the level of satisfaction with the results, and how poor results can be a doorway into investigating habits, attitudes, beliefs, and actions that produce the results.

Basic Coaching Principles

Undergirding Christian coaching are several key principles. These principles help distinguish coaching from other disciplines, such as counseling, mentoring, and consulting (see appendix 1, "Distinctions of Coaching," p. 125 for more information on these distinctions). The underlying truth of these principles for Christian coaching will become evident as they are woven through the pages of this book.

Principle 1–Taking Intentional Action

Coaching always encourages intentional action. The wise coach encourages others to continually think ahead, move forward, and be proactively involved with their lives. The wise coach looks for ways to encourage continual forward motion and intentional action. Simple questions that encourage intentional action include:

- "How can this conversation help you move forward?"
- "What specific actions are needed right now?"
- "What other options need to be considered before you take action?"
- "With that outcome in mind, what actions will you take?"

■ ■ ■ For many years, Susan felt led to pursue a master's degree in organizational development. She loved school, so the thought of it excited her. However, life kept intervening. She married, started her career, and gave birth to twins. Then she heard about coaching. The idea of receiving coaching was intriguing, particularly because the thought of getting her organizational development degree was still in her mind.

Susan decided to explore getting a coach. After interviewing several coaches, Susan hired Loren, a coach in another state. Early in their telephone coaching relationship, Loren wondered out loud what it would take for Susan to look into a degree program. "Susan, what actions can you take to start the process?"

Susan responded with several possible actions that would help her to know what was available.

"And what actions will you do first?"

Again, Susan became clear on how to prioritize the actions.

On their next call, Susan excitedly reported that she had discovered a great distance-learning program that combined on-line classes with group activities. She had already signed up for a conference call that would explain more about the program.

Loren immediately acknowledged what Susan had done and the level of enthusiasm that he heard. He then asked, "What are the next actions, now that you have a possibility in mind?"

Susan thought for a minute and responded, "I need to talk with my manager and find out if this is something my company will pay for and if I can take the time that I'll need every now and then for group projects. I also want to start thinking about how this will impact my family."

Loren responded, "How can you do school and continue to be a great wife and mother?"

Within two months, Susan had a plan for her master's degree and was enrolled in a program. She and her husband were talking about how to have the least impact on her family, and her manager had assured her that she could take the time she needed to do the project work. Susan was thrilled! ■

Principle 2–Serving

Coaching is about being in service to others, always keeping the other person's best interests in mind. Jesus modeled service by laying down His life for us. "For even the Son of Man did not come to be served, but to serve, and to give his life as a ransom for many" (Mk. 10:45).

A coach serves the person being coached by saying something difficult for the person to hear, asking the person to stretch in ways not done before, or challenging the person to see something from a totally different perspective.

In the spirit of service, the coach must also be willing to let go of the person being coached, or give a referral to someone else. For example, it might become clear that a professional service other than coaching is appropriate for the person being coached. Or, it might become clear that the person being coached would benefit from working with a different coach. In either case, keeping in mind an attitude of serving the person being coached, the coach may need to make a referral.

■ ■ ■ Several years ago, Sarah, a new executive coach, received a call asking if she could coach a ministry leader and his team as they launched a new ministry in Los Angeles. Sarah was thrilled. It would be a twelve-month contract. However, a few hours after the initial call, Sarah thought of a colleague who was closer in proximity and had experience in launching similar ministries. On one hand, this was the type of work Sarah wanted to do; on the other hand, Sarah's colleague was more suited to the project. After praying about the situation, Sarah called her colleague to see if he was interested and had time to take on a client like this. He did. Sarah knew that this was the right decision for the ministry, even though it meant giving a referral rather than taking on the client herself. ■

If coaching is about serving, then it means trusting that God is our source and our provider, rather than trusting an organization or person as our source. It means always keeping in mind the best interests of the person being coached, rather than the coach. As the apostle Paul wrote, "Do nothing out of selfish ambition or vain conceit, but in humility consider others better than yourselves. Each of you should look not only to your own interests, but also to the interests of others. Your attitude should be the same as that of Christ Jesus" (Phil. 2:3–5).

Think about It

+ Who is your source?
+ How does this impact the way you serve others?
+ How does this show up in the ways you conduct yourself?

Principle 3—Speaking the Truth in Love, without Making Others Wrong

One non-negotiable Christian coaching principle is to not make others wrong. Even when it is important to speak honestly to the person being coached, the Christian coach does not make others wrong.

The Christian coach who inadvertently makes a person being coached wrong can, and in fact should, immediately apologize and ask forgiveness. What a model this is for all of life! How many of us have people in our lives who are sensitive enough to recognize when an offense occurs and who are willing to apologize and learn from the situation?

Christian coaches must be willing to say, "I'm sorry," as soon as necessary, to learn from their mistakes, and to monitor their words carefully. The apostle Paul's words to the Ephesians offer good guidance to the Christian coach: "Do not let any unwholesome talk come out of your mouths, but only what is helpful for building others up according to their needs, that it may benefit those who listen" (Eph. 4:29).

■ ■ ■ Kiera and her coach, Todd, had been working together for several months. Recently, they had been discussing a challenge that Kiera was having with her manager, Matt. Todd assumed that Kiera needed one more conversation with Matt and said to Kiera, "You're not ready for the conversation yet." Following the comment, Todd noticed a silence that was unusual for their working relationship. He asked if he had said something that had offended her.

She responded, "Yes, it sounds like you don't think that I'm ready to talk with Matt."

Todd immediately said, "I truly am sorry that I offended you."

Later in the day, Todd thought back on the conversation and realized that he had *assumed* that she wasn't ready, rather than checking in with her. He decided to call her. "Kiera, I realized that I made an assumption that you weren't ready to talk with Matt. My error. I should have asked you if you were ready or what else you needed before you had the conversation. Again, it was my error. I hope the conversation goes really well." ■

One of the best gifts a coaching relationship offers is the gift of safety. This doesn't imply that the coach isn't honest or direct but rather implies that the coach carefully matches the words, tone, and directness to the person being coached and the situation. Safety, therefore, comes from knowing that the coach will be honest, will not intend to make the other person wrong, and will take responsibility if a mistake is made.

Not making others wrong is a huge part of creating a safe environment, or sanctuary, for people to explore and try new behaviors. Most people have few, if any, places to try to do things differently without fear of embarrassment or humiliation if a mistake is made. Very few people have any safe places at all—not at school or work and, unfortunately, usually not in churches or homes. Sometimes, the coaching relationship is the only situation in which a person knows he or she has no need to worry if mistakes are made and feels safe enough to try new behaviors.

Author Dinah Maria Mulock Craik expressed beautifully the sentiment of sharing a sanctuary with another individual when she wrote:

> Oh the comfort, the inexpressible comfort of feeling safe with a person, having neither to weigh thoughts nor measure words, but pouring them all right out, just as they are—chaff and grain together—certain that a faithful hand will take and sift them, keep what is worth keeping, and with the breath of kindness blow the rest away.[8]

Principle 4–The Power of Great Questions

Part of the beauty of coaching is the core belief that the person being coached has the answers, whether on the surface or buried. A clear distinction of Christian coaching is that we can trust God and others to come up with the needed answers. In coaching, the focus is on asking great questions that will unlock the answers rather than on giving the answers. The person being coached, rather than the coach, is responsible for answers or solutions.

Believing that answers lie within the person being coached and that person's connection with the Lord unleashes creativity and innovation. Asking questions such as, "What else are you considering?" or, "What other ideas do you have?" communicates that the person being coached knows more than is being said and is capable of coming up with more creative ways of approaching the situation. This approach subtly trains the person

---

[8]Dinah Maria Mulock Craik, *A Life for a Life* (Whitefish, Mont.: Kessinger, 2004), 184.

being coached to ask the same questions internally, increasing self-confidence and trust in God to reveal His will and purposes.

Principle 5–Coaching Isn't for Every Situation!

Coaching is appropriate in many life situations; however, in other situations, it is inappropriate. When a person honestly doesn't know what to do, coaching is inappropriate.

> ■ ■ ■ Several years ago, a team member needed to be fired, and the manager had never fired anyone before. In addition, the company risked a lawsuit if the personnel issue was handled improperly. The manager contacted his human resources (HR) professional for help in determining how to proceed. If the HR professional had tried to coach the manager through the process, precious time would have been wasted. Instead, the HR professional gave specific instruction on exactly what to do. The difficult task was completed efficiently and correctly. Giving direction was the appropriate way to work with the manager based on the manager's level of knowledge and experience. ■

Coaching is also inappropriate in situations in which information that others don't have needs to be shared. If a team member has been on vacation and doesn't know what progress has been made on an important project since the previous week, it is not wise for the manager to ask, "What do you think has happened?" Instead, a simple update is more appropriate.

Likewise, in crisis situations, clear and direct instruction is appropriate. In a burning building, it would be important to speak directly, "Get out now!" and give orders on how to evacuate the building rather than casually asking, "What do you want to bring with you as we leave the building?" Crisis situations or instances when an immediate decision is needed are not times for coaching.

While coaching is inappropriate in some settings, coaching is perfect in a number of settings. For example, coaching is a good fit when
  1. a person is ready for the next level of development personally or professionally
  2. specific goals or tasks need to be accomplished
  3. a person demonstrates a desire to respond to change positively
  4. development is as important, or more important, than the task or goal
  5. there's a sense of a new season of life and it's time to prepare

The Origins of Coaching

Coaching has existed for decades, with a variety of names. Athletic coaching is probably the best known, with many models of helping athletes move forward. Notable are Olympic coaches who strive to instill in their protégés the skills, insights, possibilities, and thought patterns needed to compete internationally. These coaches are often seen on the sidelines, cheering for their protégés as they compete, embracing and congratulating them when they win, or consoling and encouraging them when they lose.

In the 1980s, Thomas Leonard, a trained financial planner, emerged on the coaching scene. As he talked with his clients, listening to their stories, he realized that individuals needed more than financial planning; they needed life planning. A brilliant and unusual man, Leonard began to talk with his clients about their lives, challenging them to live their lives in a different way. Sometimes he might talk with a person about making dramatic changes, such as moving into a smaller living space and curtailing all expenses other than the basics. At other times, he might challenge a person to address personal needs so that values would drive behavior. Whatever Leonard was doing, it worked!

Out of Leonard's experiences came the concept of coaching others via the telephone, as it provided a level of intimacy without the challenges of face-to-face communication. He also started training others through "Coach U," using the telephone as the primary vehicle for classes. This opened other areas around the world to coach training, and Coach U remains one of the world's largest personal coach training programs.[9] Sandy Vilas took over Coach U from Leonard and continues to lead the company. Simultaneously, some of Leonard's protégés began to enlarge the coaching profession in a variety of ways. Laura Whitworth and Henry Kimsey-House launched Coach Training Institute,[10] a respected coach training school. Today, many coach-training companies target any number of coaching niches.

In 1995, the ICF was created. This organization offers professional certification for individuals as well as accreditation for coach training schools. The ICF is known for its focus on setting and maintaining high standards of professionalism. In February 1996, *Newsweek* published an article, "Need a Life? Get a Coach,"[11] which brought widespread interest in coaching. Since then, coaching has been spotlighted in thousands of articles as well as radio and television interviews.

In recent years, academic institutions have begun to offer coaching courses. Several respected universities offer coaching certification programs aligned with ICF requirements. More academic curriculum is expected to emerge in the coming years.

Right around 2000, coaching emerged in the Christian community. The Christian Coaches Network and coach training schools provide resources for Christian coaches. Gary Collins, well-known in the Christian counseling field, wrote one of the first Christian Coaching books.[12]

---

[9]Coach U can be accessed at www.coachu.com.

[10]Coach Training Institute can be accessed at www.thecoaches.com.

[11]Kendall Hamilton, "Need a Life? Get a Coach," *Newsweek* (February 5, 1996): 48.

[12]Collins, *Christian Coaching*.

In recent years, coaching has gained momentum in the Christian community. Denominational leaders discovered they could impact congregations and their leaders through coaching. Subsequently, congregational coaches started to emerge and be trained. Seminaries are beginning to see the vision of how ministers and others coming through theological academia can use coaching. Leaders at Western Seminary in Portland, Oregon, saw the potential for coaching in ministers and launched the first coaching credential program in a theological education institution in the United States. Other seminaries and academic institutions are recognizing the potential of coaching and are beginning to make coach training available to students and alumni.

Interest is continuing to escalate as people are sharing how coaching is making a difference and changing their lives. As coaching continues to emerge, the horizon is bright for Christian coaching and its transformational potential for individual believers, congregations, and even denominations.

Prayer

Lord, we submit to You and are excited about how You are leading us. Show us Your ways as we engage in the learning process. Show us how You want us to serve others. Show us how to lean on You as we seek to become more effective in all of our interactions, and remind us to continually give You all the credit and the glory. In Jesus' name, Amen.

Beyond the Book

1. How will you describe coaching when someone asks what it is?
2. What has contributed to strong relationships for you? How can you establish strong relationships quickly?
3. Look at the examples of coaching in this chapter. Think about what you would do as the coach in each situation. Think also about the approach you would take when you discuss it with the client.
4. In what areas of your life are you not taking intentional action? What steps can you take immediately to move forward?
5. What personal areas need further development so that you can focus more deeply on serving others?
6. How often do you make people feel wrong or believe that you have better answers than the other person? What can you do to make positive changes in these areas?

2

Core Coaching Skills

■ ■ ■ Forty people had registered for a class to learn basic coaching skills. When Dawn volunteered to be coached in front of the room, no one expected her to share in such depth; and no one expected her to walk out the door in such pain. The assignment for the class was to practice two basic coaching skills with Dawn: listening and asking precise questions. That's all. Yet those two skills took Dawn in an unexpected direction, and then it was time to break for lunch.

Immediately after lunch, Dawn asked to share something with the class. Hesitantly she said, "When I left for lunch, I felt like I had made a mistake by sharing the challenge that I have right now. The way you all listened and your questions made me think in ways that were painful. I didn't go to lunch with anyone because I was in too much pain. During lunch, I realized for the first time that I have choices and that there is a way through this challenge. I feel stronger than I have felt in a long time and ready to tackle the obstacles. Thank you." ■

Basic Coaching Skills

Wise coaches use a variety of skills. Two of the most powerful coaching skills are listening and asking precise questions. These two skills are the heart and soul of coaching, comprising approximately 50 percent of the coaching conversation. Wise coaches have mastered and continuously develop these two skills rather than skipping lightly over them to get to the other skills. Wise coaches know precisely when and how to use these two skills.

In addition to listening and asking precise questions, coaches use a variety of skills. Each is related in some way to listening and asking precise questions. The eight vital coaching skills covered in this book are:

Core Coaching Skills

1. Listening
2. Asking precise questions

Essential Coaching Skills

3. Identifying action
4. Delivering direct messages

Supporting Skills

5. Acknowledging
6. Sharing self
7. Being silent
8. Synthesizing

Each of these eight skills is vital because each contributes to the life or vitality of the coaching relationship. These skills can be organized in concentric circles, with the most important skills being in the core, essential skills in the next circle emanating from the core, and supporting skills in the outer circle. When a coach tosses the proverbial pebble into the pond of a coaching relationship, the first two skills rippling forth are core skills without which a relationship could not be developed. Emanating quite naturally from the initial point of the birthed relationship are essential and supporting skills, which help to deepen and strengthen the coaching conversation.

Listening and asking precise questions are the core skills. Excellence in listening and asking questions is the foundation for all other coaching skills. Identifying action and delivering direct messages are essential skills, used commonly in the coaching relationship. Wise coaches use these skills regularly and understand their power. Acknowledging, sharing self, being silent, and synthesizing are supporting skills. These skills may not be used in every coaching situation but can often be used effectively.

In the tree diagram of the Christian coaching relationship (p. 11), all eight skills are part of the relationship that branches out between the coach and person being coached. The skills, used individually or in combination with one another in coaching conversations, help the coach and person being coached to connect deeply, focus on specific topics, promote learning and discovery, establish actions, and review the conversations. However, branches do not grow without roots. A part of the coach's responsibility is to develop the personal "root system" to help the relationship branch out in God's intended direction. The wise coach will participate in training, develop the skills, gain the experience, and prepare adequately as a part of the essential commitment to the person being coached.

Foundational Coaching Skills

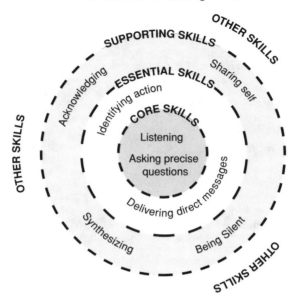

Spending time on the core coaching skills builds a strong foundation for development of the other skills. Great coaching is built on the foundation of listening intently to understand fully what is going on and asking precise questions to promote discovery for the person being coached. Because of the foundational nature of listening and asking precise questions to great coaching, these two skills will be explored in this chapter. The other six skills will be explored in the next chapter.

Think about It:

✦ As you start to look at the coaching skills, consider putting down the book at various times and practicing the skills, even in noncoaching situations. Some of the skills, such as listening, will seem simple or mundane. Very true!

✦ Even so, take this coaching challenge: For ten minutes during an upcoming conversation, try each skill intentionally. Notice what you learn about yourself and about coaching as you are practicing.

✦ Notice what happens to the other person. Remember, as you practice, you are doing exactly what you want the people you coach to do— practice skills, try on new behaviors, seek new perspectives, learn!

These skills can transform not only coaching relationships but other relationships as well!

Skill 1–Listen

Nearly two thousand years ago James, most likely the brother of Jesus, penned these words, "Everyone should be quick to listen, slow to speak" (Jas. 1:19). His ancient words, written to first-century Christians, could have been written directly to Christian coaches today!

Have you ever examined a stained-glass window at different times of the day? In the first morning light, at noon, and as the day draws to a close, different aspects of the window and its beauty are revealed. So it is with listening. The many different facets of listening can be examined at different times and in different circumstances, with the full and intricate beauty of true listening still to be revealed.

Staying Present and Focused

Two facets of listening are abundantly clear with the light of each new day. They are the ability to stay present and the ability to stay focused. Most people, whether executives in meetings, mothers with children, or parishioners sitting in pews on Sunday mornings, have trouble simply being present and focused when someone (other than themselves!) is talking. Wise coaches who want to sharpen their listening skills can begin with an intense emphasis on being present and focused.

▪ ▪ ▪ When Sam was learning to be a Christian coach, the first skill he heard about was listening. Ho hum. Sam was bored because his background was in the mental health field, and he had had numerous academic courses on listening. Still, something piqued his interest as he heard about listening this time. While other classes had discussed active listening, in which the listener summarized, clarified, and reflected back what was heard, this class focused on the listener being present and focused.

During one of the skill practices, Sam became aware of how often his mind wandered when he was "listening." Because he was a busy man and very task-oriented, he realized that he also consistently moved into solutions to keep the conversation moving forward.

While still in the class, Sam decided to listen more intently to his wife when he went home and to continue the behavior for at least a month to see the difference. He recognized this as a challenge and came up with ways to refocus his mind when it wandered. Just to get started, he decided that he would turn off the television and put down the newspaper when his wife was present in a room with him.

A few minutes after arriving home, Sam sat with no newspaper or television and let his wife talk. Still, he found his mind thinking of other things as his wife spoke. He refocused. He continued to listen at a deeper level and withheld problem-solving or sarcastic comments. For several weeks, he continued his new behaviors. One day, Sam's wife asked him to join her on the sofa. Sam had no idea what to expect and was surprised to hear her say, "I've been thinking a lot about these past few weeks. Something is different, and it's subtle. I finally figured out what it is. You've been listening to me like you never did before. I feel like I have a new husband, and I love it!" ■

Almost every adult has had a class that includes listening. Listening is a skill that is discussed and taught repeatedly, yet it is not always put into practice. The many demands of our busy lives as well as the surround-sound type world that we all live in provide explanations but not excuses for our collective case of "listening deficit disorder." How many times have you motioned for someone to come into your office while you were on the telephone, or "listened" to your child share a school problem while you were trying to balance the checkbook, or made a "to do" list while sitting in a class? Listening is a powerful skill that benefits both the coach and the person being coached.

Think about It: ———————————————————————————

✦ How many times have you been in a class that has focused on listening?

✦ How well do you really listen, even in those classes on listening?

✦ What did you put into practice from those classes?

If you're like many people interested in coaching, you think that listening is ho-hum. In actuality it's much more challenging than expected! Take this simple listening challenge:

- Find someone with whom you can talk for just three minutes, either in person or on the telephone. Find a stopwatch or timer that you can set for three minutes.
- Ask the person to discuss anything–perhaps a challenge, a plan, a dream–for three minutes while you listen. You can only listen. No talking! Ready?
- Set the timer and take three minutes to quiet your mind and listen. Just be present and focused on the other person. Go!
- What did you notice about yourself as you were listening?
- What were you thinking about as you listened?
- What did you learn about yourself, about coaching, and about the person who was talking?

Fighting Distraction

Most people realize that they're thinking of many other things when they're "listening." They're thinking about their "to do" list, the calls they need to make, the groceries they need to buy, the bills that need to be paid today, the solution to the problem that's being discussed, or a personal story that relates to what is being shared. Regardless of what you were thinking about, if you were distracted, what can you do about it? How can you set those distractions aside so that you can be totally present and focused on what is being said by the other person? You may want to try this "simple" listening activity again and reel in your mind so you can be present and focused.

Coaching requires the coach to be present and focused. Setting aside all distractions is part of being present. People have different things that distract them. For some, it's the sound of incoming e-mail or the telephone. For others, it's a "to do" list or the calls that need to be made before the end of the day. For others, it's the stack of papers on the side of the desk or the computer screen that beckons.

The wise coach is not only aware of personal distractions but also is knowledgeable about how to set them aside. For some coaches, simply turning off the telephone ringer and shutting down the computer can take care of the distractions. For others, it's writing down the shopping list or turning away from a messy desk. Since being focused on the other person and on what is being said is critical in coaching, distractions mean that the coach is off track. Whenever distractions occur, whether early in a coaching conversation or in the middle of it, it is important to be able to self-correct by refocusing on the person being coached. The wise coach is willing to let the person being coached know of the distraction and to ask for a moment to take care of it. This not only allows the coach to be present but also models for the person being coached a way of handling distractions in a transparent way.

Think about It: _____

+ What top five distractions keep you from being completely focused on what another person is saying? Each person's list will be as unique as the person making the list.

+ What can you do personally to minimize each of these distractions?

Learning to Concentrate

Coaching requires the coach to be totally focused on what's being said. One way to practice this is to concentrate on what is being said *while* another person is saying it. As the other person is speaking, speak the same words in your head (or out loud if you dare!). See if you can say every word that is being said at the same time. This means that as the other person is speaking, you are attempting to say each word at the same time. This helps to bring you back to focusing and being present when coaching.

Try this activity:

Say each word in your head as another person is speaking:
• When you are listening to the radio.
• When you are on the phone.
• When you are face to face.
• With your eyes closed (not while you're driving, please!).
• With your eyes open.

As you are present and focused when listening, you may say some things to help others expand their thoughts. For example, consider the following as ways of showing that the coach is listening and believes that there is more to say:
• "What else are you thinking about with this?"
• "And…?"
• "Wow…"
• "Hmmm…"
• "Say more…"

Although these may sound like simple, even trite, phrases, they acknowledge that the coach is listening and encourage the person being coached to continue sharing.

Avoiding Self-referencing

The goal with listening is to focus on the person being coached. Be aware of not self-referencing. None of the comments above included any references to self. A self-reference might be, "Tell me more about that," or, "I'd like to know more." Since coaching focuses on the person being coached, the purpose of encouraging more sharing is for the benefit of the person being coached, not for the benefit of the coach. Therefore, saying, "Say more about that," rather than, "Tell me more about that," makes a difference by focusing on the person being coached rather than on the coach. This is a fine distinction, yet it is powerful because it focuses more on the need of the person being coached to discover than on the need of the coach to know.

Try the following strategy in your everyday conversations:

As you practice being present and focused, remove all self-references (comments that include "me" or "I") from the conversation. Focus only on the person being coached. Write down your perceptions of the difference it makes.

In the following coaching conversation, the coach is present and focused. The italicized words represent what might be going through the coach's mind as the conversation progresses.

Coach: Chris, what would you like to talk about today?

Chris: I've had a situation come up at work that has me baffled. I don't really know what to do. I work with a person who doesn't like me. She has been ignoring me for months, but I've been able to keep doing my work. Last week she said something to our manager that wasn't even true.

Coach: Hmmm… *(There's probably more that needs to be shared.)*

Chris: She told Tom that I hadn't completed a project, but I had finished it earlier in the week. I can't figure out what to do, and I'm really angry.

Coach: Wow. *(I want to ask about the anger, but I'm not going to because I need to stay out of the way to see where Chris takes the conversation.)*

Chris: I really want to talk with Tom about it, but I also feel like I should talk with her first.

Coach: And… *(This is great because Chris is coming up with ideas already! So glad I didn't ask about the anger because it might have taken us off track.)*

Chris: If I talk with Tom first, I'm afraid that he'll get the wrong idea and that it will make the situation worse. If I talk with her about it, I have no idea what to expect.

Coach: Say more about that. *(I know that Chris can solve this without me if I keep prodding and trusting that Chris has the answers.)*

Notice in the example that the coach stayed out of the way by encouraging Chris to keep talking, clarifying and expanding the conversation. It's entirely possible that Chris came to a great solution just by talking about it. Notice, too, that Chris mentioned feeling anger. When the coach said, "Wow," Chris could have said more about being angry. If the coach had asked about it, the conversation could have gone off on a tangent, which clearly wasn't the direction Chris wanted to go.

Notice also the lack of self-references by the coach. Wise coaches know how to keep the focus and attention on the person being coached by being present and by minimizing the number of self-references.

What would that same conversation look like if the coach had not been focused and present? What if the coach had continually referenced himself?

Coach: Chris, what would you like to talk about today?

Chris: I've had a situation come up at work that has me baffled. I don't really know what to do. I work with a person who doesn't like me. She has been ignoring me for months, but I've been able to keep doing my work. Last week she said something to our manager that wasn't even true.

Coach: Man, if there is one thing that drives me nuts, it's when people say things that aren't true about me, like one time my wife told her mother that I never listen to her.

Chris: Anyway, back to me. She told Tom that I hadn't completed a project, but I had finished it earlier in the week. I can't figure out what to do, and I'm really angry.

Coach: Tell me more about how angry you are.

Chris: I really want to talk with Tom about it, but I also feel like I should talk with her first.

Coach: Well, you know, if she's a liar, I just don't think it will do any good to talk to her.

Chris: If I talk with Tom first, I'm afraid that he'll get the wrong idea and that it will make the situation worse. If I talk with her about it, I have no idea what to expect.

Coach: I think you've got problems, buddy, but I've got a dentist appointment, and I've got to run *(cell phone starts to ring)*.

Although the example is obviously exaggerated, the point is clear. People, even coaches, have a seemingly natural tendency to allow their minds to wander and to interject themselves into any situation. As with any skill, practice makes perfect. Practice staying focused and present in coaching conversations. Learn to notice when your mind wanders or when you start hearing "I" or "me" statements coming from your lips. Notice, make adjustments, and keep practicing!

Tips for Great Listening

* Maintain eye contact when face to face.
* Reduce visual distraction, especially when on the phone.
* Put phones and e-mails on silent mode so they don't intrude on the conversation.
* Determine ways to reduce mental distractions.
* Allow for silences instead of immediately jumping in with something.
* Be aware when you are interrupting...stop it!
* Relax and pay attention to all that is being said.
* If necessary, take notes to stay focused and to remember details.
* Take two to three minutes of quiet time before you are called on to be an active and present listener. Take a few deep breaths, say a prayer, and determine what will help you to be ready to listen.

According to Terry Bacon and Karen Spear, "Listening is largely a matter of patience and focus. You have to be patient enough to release your agenda and be with the client while you are coaching and focused enough to minimize distractions and truly hear what the other person is saying."[1]

---

[1]Terry Bacon and Karen Spear, *Adaptive Coaching* (Palo Alto, Calif.: Davies-Black, 2003), 165.

Listening in Three Ways

In essence, the coach is listening simultaneously in three ways.

First, the coach is listening to self to practice self-management and be an effective coach. The coach listens to self for:

- *precise questions* that need to be asked ("She just mentioned 'succeeding as a parent.' I need to ask her what that would look like.")
- *reminders* to suspend judgment ("I just had a red flag go up when he mentioned meeting with his elders. That flag is from my story, not his. What's been true in my story is not necessarily true in his. Let's see where this goes.")
- *commentary* on what is being said ("That's the third time she's speculated on leaving her current job. Each time she seems to be getting more confident in the way she says it.")

The wise coach will train this internal voice to serve the client rather than act as a distraction. The key is not for the coach to turn off the internal voice, but to use it in total service to the client.

Second, the coach must listen to the person being coached. The coach listens to the actual content of what is being shared. Beyond this, the coach listens for the meaning behind what is said, the gaps or assumptions in what is said, and even to what is not being said. The coach also listens to the person being coached by listening to the relationship itself. Listening to the relationship requires that the coach:

- consider what is being shared and how it relates to what was shared in the past
- listen for trends that can be discerned based on what has been shared
- notice when the person being coached shares a radically new thought or steers the conversation in an abrupt direction
- take note of the client's energy level, pace of conversation, mood, and other factors that "go beyond words"

Finally, along with listening to self and listening to the person being coached, the Christian coach also listens for the still, small voice or the "gentle whisper" of the Lord (1 Kings 19:12). The wise coach can enter each coaching conversation prayerfully and expectantly, prepared to hear and respond to holy "nudges" from the Holy Spirit.

Summary—Great Coaching Requires Listening in Three Ways

- The coach listens inwardly in an effort to self-manage and be in total service to the client.
- The coach listens to the person being coached, focusing on what is said and what is not said—energy, body language, tone of voice, and flow of the conversation.
- The coach listens to the Holy Spirit for insights, intuitions, and revelation that cannot come from words alone.

Skill 2–Ask Precise Questions

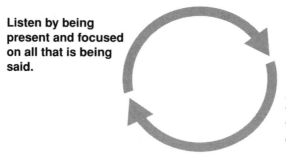

Listen by being present and focused on all that is being said.

Ask precise questions that are directly related to what is being discussed.

"Who do you say I am?" (Mt. 16:15).

Do you think Jesus could have asked a more precise, focused question? From that simple question came a profound answer that turned the life of Simon Peter, a simple fisherman, upside down and prepared the way for the launch of the Christian church. Precise questions fuel coaching conversations, causing people to think innovatively and act purposefully.

The art of asking precise questions is a learned skill. Asking questions is relatively easy. Asking precise questions is not. "Precise" implies that the question is directly related to the conversation. Precise questions result from the coach being present and focused while listening. Precise, in the coaching conversation, also means that the question promotes discovery and encourages intentional action.

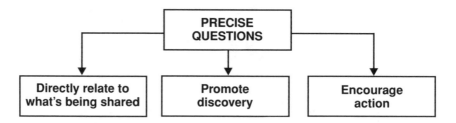

Questions Not to Ask

Questions should not be asked to satisfy the coach's curiosity or for information that the coach wants or needs. This may sound simple, but many times a coach asks questions for the wrong reason. Some questions force the person being coached into the past rather than maintaining focus on where the person wants to go. Some require the person to repeat information or to share information unrelated to the situation at hand. Some are off track. The key is to keep the questions focused on moving the person being coached forward into purposeful, intentional action.

During a keynote address in San Francisco several years ago, the speaker asked everyone to partner with another person and to only ask questions that started with "What?" Leigh turned to her partner, a man whom she had never met. As she shared a situation, the man asked several questions:

- What did you do next?
- What were you thinking?
- What else was going on?
- What finally happened?

At the end of the activity, Leigh realized that she felt very unsatisfied with the way the conversation had gone. As she thought about it, she realized that each question was for her partner's benefit, not for hers. His questions smacked of curiosity rather than moving Leigh forward. If he had been asking questions that were for her benefit, they would have sounded much different:

- What are you thinking of doing next?
- What else could you do?
- What other ways of thinking about this might help?
- What would you like to happen as an outcome?

Questions That Move a Person Forward

Well-placed, precise questions in a coaching conversation help the person being coached move forward. Questions that are based on focused listening, that are worded carefully, and that are well-timed can catapult a person forward in discovery and action. Both discovery and action are vital to the coaching process.

Each question must be asked individually rather than stacked on another question. An example of inefficient stacking is, "What do you think you should do? What do you want to do next? How will you proceed?" In this example, all are asked as one question, which can confuse the person being coached and cause that person to be unsure about which question to answer. A stronger way is to ask one question at a time. If you fear you may forget your questions if you don't ask them the moment they pop into your head, then jot them down.

Characteristics of Precise Questions

1. *Direct.* They are clear, succinct, and simple so they can be easily understood.
   - What would you like to discuss right now?
   - What next steps will you take after this conversation?

2. *Non-critical.* They are neither judgmental nor negative.
   - How will you evaluate the risk of going in this direction?
   - In what other ways might you interpret this situation?

3. *Clean.* They are free of underlying motives.
   • What resources do you have as you make this decision?
   • How can you leverage this learning with others?

4. *Deliberate.* They keep the person being coached moving forward.
   • What are the next steps?
   • By when will you take that action?

Most precise questions start with "What" or "How" These words keep the conversation open and expand the thinking and dialogue. "When?" can also be a useful question, especially toward the end of a coaching conversation as the person being coached reviews actions and commitments. These questions are considered "open-ended." What makes them distinct is their direct relatedness to the conversation and to moving the person being coached forward.

One question to be avoided is, "Why?" This simple three-letter word can create defensiveness and take a person into the past, into guilt, or into justifying and defending a position. In coaching conversations, it is best to avoid "Why?" and to find other ways to ask for the same information. For example, instead of, "Why did you decide to take that action?" you might ask, "What were the reasons behind that action?" or "What thoughts did you have when you were deciding to take that action?" These replace "Why?" and are direct, noncritical, clean, and deliberate.

Think about It: ⎯⎯⎯⎯⎯⎯⎯⎯⎯⎯⎯⎯⎯⎯⎯⎯⎯⎯⎯⎯

✦ Focus on asking "What?" and "How?" questions.

✦ Avoid "Why?"

✦ Notice what happens when you stop asking, "Why?"

Questions to Expand and Focus

If people are responding to questions with short answers, including "yes" or "no," questions may need to be asked differently. Switch from questions that start with, "Do you...," or, "Is it...," or, "Can you...," to questions that begin with "What" and "How" to expand the learning or focus the person on action. For example:

From: Do you have any ideas?
To: What ideas do you have?

From: Is it the right time for this decision?
To: How will you know it's the right time for this decision?

From: Can you see the next steps you'll take?
To: What are the next steps you'll take?

All great and precise questions are built on focused listening. The two skills go hand-in-hand.

A Starter List of Precise Questions

Having a list of precise questions that continually move people forward can be helpful. Below is only a starter list of such questions. Notice that they are direct, noncritical, clean, and deliberate.

- What outcome do you want from this coaching conversation?
- Where would you like to focus?
- How does that decision/action fit with your values?
- Are we on the right track with this conversation, or is there a better focus?
- What would be most useful to discuss right now?
- What are you willing to do next?
- What else? (Always ask for more than one response so the person has choices.)
- What's the first step you'll take? By when?
- What obstacles do you anticipate? How will you overcome them?
- What do you need in order to succeed?

Think about It:
✦ Add to this list fifteen questions that are useful for you. The first five may come easily. The last ten may require thoughtful effort.

✦ Keep this list and add to it until you have a list of questions that you can rely on when needed.

✦ Be sure to keep the questions short and simple rather than complicated.

A great question at this point might be: "What's the benefit in asking questions rather than telling a person what to do, especially if you think you have a great idea? Seriously, what's the benefit?"

Asking questions of the person being coached in a coaching relationship, rather than telling the person being coached what to do, offers many benefits:

- The person being coached becomes a source of great ideas! For many people, this is a real "aha" moment!
- The person being coached feels a deeper level of ownership of taking action if that person initiates the idea. Ownership builds commitment.
- The person being coached is empowered to be more creative and innovative.
- The person being coached experiences an increased level of self-trust and belief as a result of the coaching.

■ ■ ■ Two days after the 9/11 terrorist attacks, David called his coach and asked for help. His company had been hit hard by the terrorist strikes, and his task was to protect one large segment of the company's infrastructure. This was not David's only concern. In David's words, "I am in a crisis right now. I am expected to be a leader for my family, my community, and my company. I don't know what to do."

Zach, David's coach, replied thoughtfully. "David, you've listed three areas of leadership that all require your attention right now. Where do you want to start?"

"I need to start with my family. My wife and daughters are terrified. Last night, we all slept in the living room in sleeping bags because everyone was so afraid."

Again, Zach responded carefully, "Starting with your family, what can you do to help them?"

David thought a moment and said, "I think we need to talk about what each person needs right now. Maybe a family meeting would help."

"And how will you start the family meeting?" asked Zach.

"First, I want to talk with my wife. I want to let her know what I'm thinking about and see if she agrees. That will help her to know that my first priority is my family."

"And then…"

"Then, I'll let the girls know that we're taking a serious look at what our family needs right now. I'll ask them what would help them feel more connected and safe." ■

Other questions that Zach asked were:

- Who else needs to be contacted?
- Where else might you go?
- What obstacles do you anticipate to this process?
- What's the best-case scenario that might come out of this?
- The worst?
- How will you handle this if it happens?

■ ■ ■ Ten days later, David and Zach talked again. David reported that during the family meeting and in the following week, the family came up with a contingency plan and took action to implement it. They purchased four cell phones, called a relative in Wisconsin and asked if they could come to stay, packed the car with emergency supplies, stocked the house with food and water, and helped a number of neighbors as they struggled through the aftermath of the attack. David's wife was so pleased with what the family had done that she shared it with other parents at her daughters' school. The principal heard about it and called a special PTA meeting, asking the family to share their contingency plan and how they were helping others.

After David shared about his family, he told Zach he was ready to focus on work. Zach, knowing nothing about technology contingency plans, asked, "Where do you need to start?" ▪

Other questions:

- What specific actions will you take?
- Who else in the company needs to be included?
- What resources will you need?
- How will you get them?
- What else?

▪ ▪ ▪ Within two weeks, David had a contingency plan in place that thwarted a dozen threats on the company systems. David's work became highly recognized, and he received a letter of commendation from the chairman of the board, which he immediately sent to Zach, thanking him for his help with the contingency plan. Zach was well aware, and pointed out to David, that David had done all the work and could take all the credit!▪

Precise questions have many beneficial results. The person being coached:

- becomes aware of something bigger and more important to address
- moves from talking to taking action
- shifts from reactive to proactive
- thinks more creatively
- feels more confident to take action
- shifts from nonbeneficial attitudes, beliefs, or perceptions to new ones that are action-oriented

As the coach and person being coached work together, they are collaborating, or co-laboring, toward a goal. Coaching is a collaborative journey toward the goals of the person being coached.

Two indispensable skills along that journey are listening and asking precise questions. Use these skills liberally! Practice as much as you can so that you can rely on both of these skills. Trust the Holy Spirit's promptings as you listen and ask precise questions. Often a simple question, prompted by the Holy Spirit, propels the person being coached forward.

Prayer

Lord, we are excited about how You are leading us. Show us how we can be more like You in our ability to listen and to ask precise questions. Help us to move away from where we are comfortable into new ways of being with others. Help us to recognize when we can improve and to be willing to learn and grow. We want to honor You and serve others through these skills. We give You all the glory and credit. In Jesus' name, Amen.

Beyond the Book

1. How willing are you to learn and grow in your ability to listen and ask precise questions?
2. What are you willing to do immediately to improve your listening and asking of precise questions by at least 50 percent?
3. How will you keep track of what you are learning and observing?
4. With whom can you practice these skills immediately?
5. What structure or accountability do you need to keep moving forward?

3

Essential and Supporting
Coaching Skills

"The rain came down, the streams rose, and the winds blew and beat against that house; yet it did not fall, because it had its foundation on the rock" (Mt. 7:25).

Sometimes storms will wreak havoc on coaching relationships. A coach may casually comment, "You're really considering that?" with an intent of playfulness, or, "You sound really pleased," when the person isn't. Any number of misunderstandings may arise in the relationship. Words can be misinterpreted. Feelings may be hurt. Progress may be slow. However, when a coaching relationship is built on the foundation of listening and asking precise questions for the sake of the client, the relationship can withstand troubled times.

Essential and Supporting Skills

Beyond the rock-solid foundation of listening and asking precise questions are six additional skills needed in Christian coaching. As mentioned earlier, two are essential skills, and four are supporting skills:

Essential Coaching Skills	*Supporting Skills*
Identifying action	Acknowledging
Delivering direct messages	Sharing self
	Being silent
	Synthesizing

Listening and asking precise questions make up approximately 50% of the coaching conversation. The remaining skills are used frequently when appropriate.

Essential Coaching Skills

Skill 1—Identifying Action

The script has been written, edited, and approved. The actors have been selected. The props have been constructed. The crew has been trained. Then, with one word, all the behind-the-scenes work comes to fruition: "Action!"

Action is always a part of coaching. Action may consist of an intentional thinking process, a writing assignment to produce more clarity, or detailed steps to be taken within an established time frame. Action is a critical component of coaching, and masterful coaches are adept at helping people to identify and take action.

Intentional action should be directly aligned with the situation being discussed. A coach is charged with the responsibility to nudge the person being coached into effective action. Who can forget the words of astronaut Neil Armstrong when he first stepped on the moon in 1969: "That's one small step for man, one giant leap for mankind." Often, what may appear to be a small step for a person being coached is actually a giant leap, propelling that person into an unimagined God-orchestrated future.

Jesus, in His three-year ministry on earth, was the master of calling people to action. He consistently called His followers to move beyond mental assent into meaningful action. Jesus urged Peter to live out his professed love for Him, "Feed my lambs" (Jn. 21:15). He urged all those within the sound of His voice, "If someone strikes you on the right cheek, turn to him the other also" (Mt. 5:39). The Christian life is a life of intentional action. The Christian coaching relationship is one of calling people to intentional action.

Action-oriented Questions

Because we are building on the foundational skills discussed in the previous chapter, listening and asking precise questions are at the heart of identifying action. Here are some action-oriented questions:

- What specifically are you going to do?
- How will you do it?
- When will you do it?
- What's the first step you will take? By when?
- What else do you need to consider as you move forward?
- Who else can be involved to help you move ahead?

Shannon: I really want to do this project differently than I've done my projects before. In the past, I've left things until too late, and then it's been crazy trying to get everything done. This is a big enough project that I want to do it differently.

Coach: Congratulations on wanting to make some changes early in the project. What specifically will you do differently, starting now?

Shannon: I can find out what the deadlines are and start to work on a timeline so I know exactly what needs to be done and by when.

Coach: What steps will you take to get the info you need?

Shannon: I need to call my manager and Colleen, another team member.

Coach: When will you talk to each person?

Shannon: I will call both this week, before Friday.

Notice in the above example that the coach is using "will" rather than "can." "Will" is a much stronger verb that "can." It has less "wiggle room." Shannon "can" do just about anything, but "will" she? With each question the coach asked, the goal was to help Shannon take intentional action aligned with her identified outcome–doing this project differently.

When encouraging the person being coached to identify action, the wise coach is specific. In the example above, the coach started by asking, "What specifically will you do differently, starting now?" This question has two elements of specificity. One is to identify the specific actions. The other is to identify that Shannon is starting now, not sometime in the future. Using phrases like "specific," "right now," "in the next day," or other detailed or explicit language helps people take action.

Think about It:

✦ List at least five additional action-oriented questions that can propel a person being coached into intentional action.

✦ What type of reply would you expect to each of these questions?

✦ What follow-up questions do you need to be ready to ask?

Meeting Resistance to Action

Occasionally, a person being coached resists taking action. How should a coach address such a situation? The coach must hold the person being coached accountable for taking action while remaining nonjudgmental. The coach can ask the person being coached to identify specific roadblocks to action.

Shannon: I didn't call my manager or Colleen last week. I just didn't have time.

Coach: Hmmm…no time? Shannon, what's really going on?

Or

Coach: Wow, that's a surprise, Shannon. You were so sure you'd make the calls. What happened?

Or

Coach: What would be best for us to discuss today to help you move forward?

All the above comments are intended to help Shannon get into action about the current subject or move forward in a different direction. Even if Shannon decides to focus elsewhere, the coach will ask Shannon to identify specific actions in the new direction.

When it comes to the coaching skill of identifying action, remember:

- The person being coached almost always comes up with the action(s). The coach is there to prod, encourage, and clarify, but not typically to suggest.
- Occasionally, the person being coached gets stuck in such a way that the coach might offer a "challenge" to promote action and forward movement. The person being coached can accept, reject, or renegotiate the challenge so that the challenge leads to a meaningful action.
- The coach encourages specific actions by helping the person being coached distinguish between goals, desires, and actions. Actions are tangible steps that can lead to goals (outcomes) and fulfill desires (hopes, wishes). For example, exercising three times each week (action) can help a person have more energy (goal) and feel better about himself or herself (desire).
- One of the few times a coach will use close-ended questions would be when it is important to clarify commitment level. For example, "You have said you will have that important conversation next Tuesday. On a scale of 1 to 10, what's your commitment to making that happen?"
- The coach prompts the person being coached to think in detail about the action(s) being taken: when it will happen, where it will happen, potential barriers to making it happen.

Skill 2—Delivering Direct Messages

■ ■ ■ When Graham was only fifteen, a friend accused him of lying, "Graham, you tell lies all the time. I never know when to believe you. I don't want to be your friend anymore." The words shocked Graham to the core. He knew his friend's words were true. He also knew that others undoubtedly recognized his lies.

Over the next few weeks, Graham's family decided to move to another community where his father would be working in a new job. When the friend heard about the move, he approached Graham again. "Graham, I've been thinking. Moving to a new town may be the best thing for you. Stop lying. Never tell another lie. You can make a fresh start."

Those two conversations changed Graham's life. He did just as his friend recommended, and he never told another lie. Twenty-five years later, he still hasn't forgotten the difficult words that changed his life. ■

Holy Scripture clearly teaches that believers are to deliver direct messages with the specific intent being to benefit the person to whom the words are spoken. The apostle Paul, in writing to the Ephesians, referred to this as, "speaking the truth in love" (Eph. 4:15).

Think about It: ————————————————————

✦ Think about a time when a direct message caused a shift in your perspective or a change in your direction.

✦ Powerful, direct messages, as part of a coaching conversation, can significantly move a person forward and propel the person in a different direction.

The Purpose of Messages

Delivering direct messages is one of the most powerful coaching skills. It is easy for some coaches and challenging for others. Messages can be in the form of statements or questions. Either way, the purpose is to assist the person being coached in moving forward quickly and more deeply than normal conversations might.

For example, when a person asks, "Do you think I can do this?" a direct message back might be, "Do *you*?" In truth, it really doesn't matter if the coach believes the person can do it or not. What matters is what the person being coached believes. By asking back to the person, "Do *you*?" the coach forces the person being coached to determine a personal set of beliefs.

A coach can use hundreds of ways to get a person's attention through delivering a direct message. The key is to deliver the message concisely.

Instead of being judgmental or critical, direct messages are

- *clean.* Be sure there's no judgment or criticism.
- *direct.* Just say it, rather than beating around the bush!
- *concise.* Use simple, short sentences–seven words or less!
- *relevant.* Be sure the message fits squarely within the flow of the conversation.
- *objective.* Focus purely on helping the person being coached move forward.

Responding to Pivotal Statements

The coach has several ways to respond to pivotal statements made by the person being coached. The example below shows a progression of direct messages from several words to just two words.

Claire: I know that I need to have it totally planned within twelve months.
Coach: twelve months is too long…
    Or
Coach: And if you wait that long…?
    Or
Coach: Do it in five months.
    Or
Coach: Five months.

Whenever a coach delivers a message, the coach always takes a risk that it might be resisted at first. This risk is mitigated when the coach allows the person being coached to either accept or reject the message.

In the earlier example about Graham and his friend, the friend took a huge risk when he delivered several direct messages. First, he said "Graham, you tell lies all the time. I never know when to believe you. I don't want to be your friend anymore." Next, several weeks later, he said, "Stop lying. Never tell another lie. You can make a fresh start."

Count the number of words in each sentence. The fewest is just two words, and the longest is nine words. All are simple, common words. Yet the impact was huge.

Standing Firm and Taking Responsibility

If a direct message offends because the person being coached doesn't want to face the reality of the situation, then the coach may need to stand firm. The wise coach knows when to apologize and when to stand firm. In the example with Graham, his friend didn't apologize, and Graham was propelled into new life.

Delivering direct messages can generate high rewards, yet risk is also involved. If a direct message is off track and offends the person being coached, the wise coach takes full responsibility for the offense and seeks forgiveness as soon as possible. The coach must be willing to say, "I'm so sorry. I didn't mean to offend you." The coach can also say, "I take full responsibility for my mistake. I apologize," or, "I am truly sorry for my words that hurt you. Will you forgive me?"

Whatever it takes, it is critical to recognize and clear up any offenses as quickly as possible. Such honest and quick action not only helps to restore the relationship, but also models a lifestyle of awareness and taking responsibility when something goes wrong.

Delivering direct messages is one of the most powerful skills when done in a way that respects and honors the person being coached. The wise coach is always ready and willing to use this skill when appropriate and to take full responsibility if the message offends.

Think about It:

✦ Recall a time when you delivered a direct message or spoke the truth in love.

✦ What was the outcome?

✦ If the outcome was not as intended, what could you do differently the next time you deliver a direct message?

Supporting Coaching Skills

Coaches will not use supporting skills in every conversation. Developing the skills will, however, serve a coach well in several critical situations. These skills are used only as needed and appropriate. They help deepen and strengthen the coaching relationship.

Skill 3–Acknowledging

What happens when people are acknowledged

- for a job well done?
- for a small step toward a larger goal?
- for a healthy change in perspective?

What happens when a coach gives acknowledgment as a way of investing and believing in the person being coached? By delivering timely and authentic acknowledgments, a trusted coach can be the catalyst that a person being coached needs to keep moving forward. "But encourage one another daily, as long as it is called Today" (Heb. 3:13a).

Think about It:

✦ When was the last time you were acknowledged for a job well done?

✦ How did it make you feel? What happened immediately afterward?

✦ When was the last time you purposefully acknowledged someone for something specific?

✦ What was the response? What happened afterward?

Benefits of Acknowledgment

Acknowledgment takes very little time or effort; yet, it reaps huge benefits. Acknowledgment inspires people to do more good thinking and more good work. People love to be acknowledged; yet, acknowledgment seems to be in short supply in today's world. A coach's acknowledgments may be the only positive reinforcements that the person being coached is receiving. Watch what happens when others are acknowledged!

It takes only a few seconds to say that a person's actions are noticed. It takes a few more seconds to write an e-mail or leave a phone message.

Components of Acknowledging

Acknowledging has three components:
1. Timing
2. Specificity
3. Style

Timing: Acknowledgments are most powerful when given as soon as possible. When a positive change takes place, when a step in the right direction is made, or when a great job is done, that's the best time for a coach to let the person know it was noticed. Be ready and willing to acknowledge as soon as the behavior is observed.

Sometimes it's not possible to give immediate acknowledgement. No worries! As soon as possible, call or e-mail the person being coached.

Specificity: Be specific when acknowledging. Be specific about what has been noticed, about the small steps taken, about a change in attitude, about a changed belief, or about anything the person being coached has done that can be genuinely acknowledged.

Instead of saying, "Great!" say, "That action sounds perfectly matched to what you're trying to achieve!" Instead of saying, "Sounds really good," say, "What you're saying shows that you've given this a lot of thought and are moving forward. Congratulations!"

Be specific when giving acknowledgments.

Style: Two points of style are important when acknowledging others. First, start acknowledgments with "you" or something other than "I." Saying, "I loved finding the report on my desk," is very different than saying, "That report you did was excellent! It was wonderful to find it this morning!" Just like prompts when listening, it is best to leave out self-referencing when acknowledging.

Think about It: _____

✦ Practice starting acknowledgments with "you" or something else other than "I."

Second, know how a person likes to be acknowledged. Does the person like public or private acknowledgment? Does the person like to see or hear the acknowledgment? An acknowledgment done in the wrong way minimizes its impact.

■ ■ ■ Allen, a retired senior pastor of a large church of more than 1,200 people, tells about a mismatch of acknowledgment. During a particularly challenging time when the church was in a building campaign, Allen coached a trusted staff member charged with overseeing the building process. Steve was to ensure that the building was designed and built to specifications, that the staff and volunteers were ready when the building was completed, and that the church continued to function administratively throughout the building campaign.

To Allen's pleasure, the building was completed successfully. Everything about it exceeded his expectations.

Allen wanted to acknowledge Steve, so he decided to throw a surprise party for him. He invited Steve's family and friends along with everyone who had played a major role in the building project. More than 300 people were waiting in a large room for Allen and Steve to make their entrance. On the big day, Allen picked up Steve, took him to lunch, and decided to "drop by" the church for a moment. When the doors swung open, and Steve appeared in the doorway, everyone yelled, "Surprise!"

To everyone's horror, Steve's eyes rolled back in his head, and he fell over backward in a dead faint. As he fell, he hit his head on a stair, leaving him unconscious and bleeding. Allen called for an ambulance, and Steve was rushed to the hospital where he received fifteen stitches and was treated for a severe concussion.

When Allen tells this story, he adds what he learned from this unfortunate event. Steve was a very private man. He hated being the center of attention. He would have loved an e-mail or a voice message from Allen congratulating him on seeing the building project through to its successful completion. Either would have been a much better acknowledgment and well matched to his style than a big and very expensive party! ■

As this story illustrates, acknowledging is a skill that must be learned, practiced, and honed for best impact. Wise coaches pay attention to how their acknowledgments land and constantly seek to improve this skill.

Tips on the Skill of Acknowledging

* Be constructive in everything that is said.
* Acknowledge small, as well as large, steps.
* Be liberal in acknowledging others. These may be the only positives that the person being coached receives.
* Focus on strengths.

❊   Always acknowledge intentional action.

❊   Be genuine in all acknowledgments. If you don't believe it, don't say it!

Skill 4–Sharing Self

To share or not to share, that is indeed the question! It takes skill for a coach to know when to share and when not to share personal information. It takes skill for a coach to share the appropriate amount of personal information. It takes skill for a coach to turn the conversation back to the person being coached after sharing something personal.

When a coach has a burning story inside that's waiting to burst out, it may or may not be the right time to share. It is, however, the right time to ask the Lord for wisdom and discernment about what is best for the person being coached. "If any of you lacks wisdom, he should ask God, who gives generously to all without finding fault, and it will be given to him" (Jas. 1:5).

A coach can use many approaches when considering sharing something personal with the person being coached:

Shannon: I am really struggling with this situation. It isn't clear for me, yet.

Coach: (*conflicted inside about sharing a similar story and deciding not to*) Shannon, you said that you are struggling. Struggling creates powerful learning. What's most useful for you right now?
   Or

Coach: (*conflicted inside about sharing a similar story and still not sure*) Shannon, I've had a similar experience, but I can't decide if this is a good time to share or not. What's best for you?
   Or

Coach: (*conflicted inside about sharing a similar story and deciding to share*) Shannon, may I share a similar experience that might be helpful to you?

If a coach is considering sharing a personal experience, asking the person being coached before sharing is a good idea. Sometimes the person being coached is so immersed in a personal situation that a coach's sharing a personal experience becomes distracting and annoying. At other times, the person being coached genuinely desires to hear a personal word from the coach and benefits from it.

A wise coach knows that sharing self is like a fine spice: a little goes a long way. For this reason, the coach keeps personal sharing reserved for just those right moments. Herein lies a warning: sharing experiences that do not fully align with what is going in the life of the person being coached reveals poor listening on the part of the coach. The moment must be just right, and when it is, sharing personal experiences can fuel the person being coached like nothing else.

Once a coach decides to share something personal, it must be concise. The amount of detail can either be too little, making the story irrelevant; too much, making the story boring or unclear; or just right. Just right means that the right amount of detail is included so that the story is relevant, clearly focused on the topic being discussed, and helps the conversation move forward.

Some people speak in paragraph format, and some speak in bullets. When sharing a personal experience, the effective coach speaks few words and then turns the conversation back to the person being coached.

Coach: May I share a similar experience?
Shannon: That would be helpful right now.
Coach: I had a situation a few years ago when something similar occurred. I had to figure out who else I could talk to because I wasn't clear. As I was deciding with whom to talk, I became clearer about the situation. Then, when we talked, I was in a much better position to move ahead. As you hear this, how is this relevant, if at all?

Regardless of what is shared, remember to share just the right amount of detail and to turn the conversation quickly back to the person being coached. Some ways of turning the conversation back to the person being coached include the following:

- "Hope that was useful. How would you like to proceed?"
- "Where do we go from here?"
- "Your situation is slightly different...."
- "As you hear this, what thoughts occur to you?"

The coach's experiences can benefit the coaching process as long as the experiences are sprinkled carefully and not used as a way of giving answers. The wise coach is willing to share examples that worked as well as mistakes that have been made. When a coach shares mistakes, the person being coached is subtly given permission to make mistakes and to learn from them. Thus, the coach is modeling how to learn from mistakes as well as sharing personal stories that are life-giving to the person being coached.

Skill 5–Being Silent

"There is a time for everything, / and a season for every activity under heaven... /a time to be silent and a time to speak" (Eccl. 3:1, 7b).

Silence is a wonderful skill that coaches rarely use! "But, I'm not hired to be quiet. I'm hired to help someone move forward." This is a common theme for coaches. Yet, what a difference strategically placed silence can make!

It has been said, "Silence is one great art of conversation." Conversations are more than words filling the air. Sometimes silence speaks more volumes than words could even dare. Author Thomas Carlyle agreed, stating, "Speech is of time, silence is of eternity."[1]

Silence is indeed "golden," even when a coach sees or hears something that needs to be mentioned. Sometimes silence allows a new thought, a different perspective, or an effective action to emerge. Sometimes a coach's brilliant comment can be perceived as an interruption.

Think about how many interruptions we create unnecessarily. Think about what it would be like to talk for even a short time, uninterrupted! Appropriate silence helps create an uninterrupted conversation.

Silence is a gift to those who are introverted because it allows them to think in a quiet environment. Silence is also a gift for those who are extroverted because it allows them to talk and to think. When an extrovert goes into thinking mode with a silent coach, it can produce tremendous awareness and action. The wise coach lets the person being coached know the role of silence so that that person can welcome the silent moments rather than assuming the silence connotes something awkward.

Tips on When to Be Silent

* After asking a powerful question
* When the person being coached is thinking through a situation and doing well without any interruptions
* After delivering a direct message
* Any time you're not sure what to say

Think about It:

+ In some of your daily conversations, try silence, even for as little as ten seconds.
+ Notice the response from the one with whom you are conversing.
+ Notice your response.
+ From your perspective, what are some benefits of silence?

To Share or To Be Silent?

It is hard to imagine two more dissimilar skills as sharing and silence. How can a wise coach know when to share self or when to be silent or when to use any of the other coaching skills? The dynamics of the coaching relationship will be explored in depth in chapter 5, but for now it may be helpful to note three keys:

First, recall that all skills are used in service to the person being coached. The "right" thing to do is to aid the person being coached in moving forward.

---

[1]Thomas Carlyle, essay on Sir Walter Scott, in *Critical and Miscellaneous Essays,* vol. 4 (Boston: Houghton, Mifflin, 1881), 190, quoted online at http://www.bartleby.com/73/1691.html.

Second, every coaching conversation is a dance. The ICF talks about "dancing in the moment" as being a competency related to coaching presence. Dancing in the moment means the coach is able to discern through subtle surveillance the intention and needs of the person being coached and provide flexible response. As the previous chapter emphasizes, such dancing requires very intense listening and focus on the person being coached as well as attention to the Holy Spirit.

Third, remember that no coaching conversation is lost on the misapplication of a skill or two. If you share when you should have been silent, simply notice the fact, add the experience to your growing inventory of coaching knowledge, and move forward as an even wiser coach.

Skill 6–Synthesizing

To synthesize means to bring all the parts together into a whole. This is a critical skill in coaching, because coaching conversations go in so many directions. Coaches who synthesize are able to track themes from different conversations (or even in the same conversation) and link them together.

Erin: I want to talk about how my mother's illness is affecting me and about some challenges at church.
Coach: Where would you like to start?
Erin: Let's talk about my mother's illness. She's really been sick, and I fear that she may die. It's been so upsetting to me because we're so close. I'm not ready for her to die.
Coach: Wow, no wonder you've had challenges at church. You've mentioned the challenges before, but you haven't really discussed all that's happening with your mother. Maybe these are linked more than you realize. What would be the best direction for us to go?

In this example, the coach brought together two different subjects: Erin's mother's illness and her challenges at her church. The coach referenced earlier conversations, suggested a link between the two, and then turned back to Erin to decide where to focus.

Wise coaches keep track of themes as they weave in and out of coaching. Coaches remember simple things that can be mentioned when appropriate. A simple comment such as, "You've mentioned before that you have had difficulty with that person," can speak loudly to the person being coached. It speaks about the coach's attention to detail, shows the coach's ability to notice and bring together different themes, and reaffirms to the person being coached that the coach is listening.

Tips for Synthesizing

✳ Take simple and brief notes that might help later in the coaching relationship or conversation.

✳ Listen for themes and patterns. For example, if a person consistently says, "Makes sense…," but doesn't take action, the coach could respond after hearing the phrase the next time, "You use the phrase 'makes sense' frequently. What exactly does it mean to you?"

✳ Keep track of the initial purpose for the coaching and refer back to it when appropriate. "When we first started talking, you mentioned wanting to 're-career.' How does this conversation fit with that?"

Beyond the Skills: Two Critical "What If's"

"What If I Get Stuck?"

When difficult situations are presented, even experienced coaches feel stuck at times and aren't sure what to say or ask. When that happens, it's a good idea to pray for God's wisdom and direction. If you are comfortable doing so, ask the person being coached if you may verbalize a short prayer. If not, utter a short, silent prayer. In addition, it can be helpful to have some questions or statements that you know are useful in times like this. Below are some examples of ways to continue moving forward, keeping the focus on the direction that best suits the person being coached:

- "Wow. You have a lot going on! What is the best focus right now?"
- "What would make this conversation most useful right now?"
- "What question would you like to be asked?"
- "What's missing in order for you to…?"
- "What do you need right now?"

As illustrated above, many statements include the words "right now." These words help to maintain focus on what is currently being discussed while encouraging people to keep moving forward. The wise coach has a number of questions or comments that can be brought into the coaching conversation when needed. In addition, skills are always important to intentionally draw on when challenges arise. Remember to use the skills of listening, asking precise questions, and acknowledging if you don't know what else to do. And, don't forget to pray!

"What If I Make a Mistake?"

There really should not be an "if" in the question above. The appropriate question is "What do I do *when* I make a mistake?" Every coach makes mistakes. Wise coaches pay attention and know when they have made a mistake. Wise coaches know how to make it right.

Sometimes a mistake calls for an apology. Be prepared to apologize! Saying, "I'm sorry," or, "I really didn't intend to offend you; please forgive me," models how mistakes can be handled well. Asking for forgiveness is scriptural. Asking for forgiveness and apologizing are healing and can help form stronger relationships while moving forward.

Sometimes a mistake means refunding money. Be prepared to talk about the mistake, take responsibility if it was the coach's error, and let the person know that a refund is on the way. Then follow up with the refund and a kind note. Sometimes this allows the person being coached to reenter the coaching relationship at a later date. The bottom line is that coaches should be prepared to take responsibility for mistakes and make them right.

Final Word on Coaching Skills

It is impossible to know what conversations will emerge when coaching. When all else fails, the core coaching skills of listening and asking precise questions serve to move the conversation forward. Practice all the skills intentionally, especially the core coaching skills. Learn and grow!

Prayer

Lord Jesus, we thank You for the ways that You listen to us and for how You work in our lives. Help us to be ever alert so that we can speak life to others and represent You well. Help us to be Your vessels and to model Your ways with all who come across our paths, especially with our families and friends. May we not only hear what they are saying, but may we also hear Your voice and sense Your direction as we respond. In Jesus' name, Amen.

Beyond the Book

1. Pay attention to how often you currently use the coaching skills. Try to increase your usage by 50 percent beginning immediately! Notice what happens.
2. Invite five people into a coaching relationship with you. Let them know that you want to practice coaching, and that you want their feedback. Then set up specific times to coach them. Be sure to ask for input at the end of each coaching conversation, and be open to learn from what is shared.
3. Listen for times when people ask to talk with you informally and when you can intentionally use one or more of the coaching skills. Notice their responses.
4. Watch for times when you say something that hurts the other person. Clean up any messes as soon as possible. Make this a lifelong journey.

4

Models for the
Coaching Conversation

Jesus was a Master Teacher. His three years with His disciples were years like no others. The Twelve walked with Him, listened to Him, watched Him, learned from Him. A pivotal teaching moment in the relationship between Jesus and His disciples came when Jesus taught them how to pray.

How would the early followers of Jesus—and other believers—have known how to turn to the Heavenly Father without a model prayer offered by Jesus? Jesus uttered the words of the Lord's Prayer (see Mt. 6:9–13; Lk. 11:2–4), the model prayer, which has given skeletal structure to the prayers of millions of believers over the course of nearly two thousand years. The Lord's Prayer, since the day that Jesus offered it, has reminded Christians of the important elements of going to the Father in prayer.

Coaching models are much like the model prayer that Jesus provided through the Lord's Prayer. As the Lord's Prayer guides believers in how to pray, coaching models guide individuals in how to coach. Models provide guidance through the coaching process so that a coach can relax into the conversation and, at the same time, remember the important elements of an effective coaching conversation.

Many coaching models are available to coaches. Wise coaches know the value of models, use elements from a variety of models, and feel free to develop their own personal model, which might include elements from several other models.

As described in chapter 1 (p. 11) the tree with its root system, branches, and fruit offers a visual for the Christian coaching relationship. This is a picture of strong, healthy coaching relationships. With that in place, coaching conversation models support the coaching relationship.

This chapter looks at three models for coaching conversations that can help a coach serve a client within a healthy coaching relationship. Rather than presenting a brand new model, this chapter acquaints the reader with several established models that can be used in combination or individually. Again, the goal is to use models as guides to assist in moving the person being coached forward with agility.

Remember, a coach uses coaching skills as a part of the coaching conversation, which is a part of the coaching relationship. These three components—skills, conversations, relationship—are separate and necessary elements in great coaching.

Each of the three models in this chapter uses the coaching skills discussed in the two previous chapters. The core skills of listening and asking precise questions are used in each phase of each model. The essential and supporting skills are used as needed and appropriate.

The Hourglass Model

Christian coach Jane Creswell created the Hourglass Model[1] to represent the shape of a coaching conversation. This model is straightforward and leaves a lasting impression because of its visual image. The wise coach knows how to incorporate all segments of the Hourglass Model in each coaching conversation.

 **Top of hourglass—clarify and focus the conversation**

Center—confirm a specific focus that is actionable

Bottom—explore, identify, and align actions with focus

Top of the Hourglass—Clarify and Focus the Conversation

When a coaching conversation begins, many subjects could be discussed. The wide part of the hourglass represents the width of possibilities. It is important to continue asking questions and helping the person being coached to gain clarity about the specific focus of the conversation. It may take up to half of each coaching conversation to determine the precise focus of the conversation.

---

[1]Jane Creswell has two thrusts with her coaching. Internal Impact reaches into the corporate world, and The Columbia Partnership touches ministries at many levels. See www.Internal–Impact.com and www.TheColumbiaPartnership.org.

Gina: So much is happening. My husband has just gotten a great job offer about two hours away, so we would need to move by the end of the year. My work is going really well, so I'm not sure I want to move right now. And our church is expanding to two services on Sundays, which means that our worship team will have to be at both services. That means a lot more time at the church for me.

Coach: Gina, you have so much going on! Where would you like to focus?

Gina: I didn't even mention that we had decided to do a major kitchen project, and I have to travel all of next month. I really need to figure out how to do all of this!

Coach: Wow. No wonder you said, "So much is happening!" So, what would be best for us to discuss right now?

Gina: I really don't know. I feel like I'm spinning!

Center–Confirm a Specific Focus That Is Actionable

As the shape of an hourglass implies, at the most narrow part, only one grain of sand can pass through at a time. This is exactly what is desired in coaching. While the top part of the model is used to identify a number of possible focal points, the goal for the center is to confirm the specific focus that is like the single grain of sand that passes through the neck of the hourglass.

A word of caution: just because one focus has been identified doesn't mean that another more specific focus won't be uncovered during the conversation. The wise coach is open to the possibility that an even more important topic will be discovered, and is flexible enough to refocus until the individual grain of sand is identified as the primary focus for the call.

Coach: As you think of all of this, what is most pressing to talk about?

Gina: I'm not really sure.

Coach: (*silence, at least for 10 seconds*)

Gina: I think I want to talk about moving. That's where I want to start because a move out of town would impact all the other issues–my church's worship team, my job, and the kitchen remodeling.

Bottom–Explore, Identify, and Align Actions with Focus

Once the most important focus area has been identified and confirmed, actions usually are easily identified. This is the time to explore many options and to determine which are most directly aligned with the specific focus of the conversation. While the person being coached is identifying options, a great question to ask is, "What else?" Ask this question many times to continue identifying additional possibilities and solutions. Once the possibilities are identified and it's time to finish the coaching conversation, the wise coach asks the person being coached to review what actions will be taken and by when. This finalizes the bottom part of the Hourglass Model.

Coach: Great place to begin, Gina! As you think about moving, where do you want to start?

Gina: (*pause*) Where we could live. I guess we could live in between our two job locations, so we'd each have an hour drive. Or we could live near Nick's work, and I could check into working from home. I probably should check into that at work, but I don't want them to know that I'm moving yet.

Coach: So, first you need to decide about where you want to live and if you have the option of telecommuting...

Gina: Actually, if telecommuting is a possibility, that will determine where we can live. I'll start checking into that first.

Coach: By when do you think you'll have more clarity on this?

Gina: I hope by Friday. I'll start with HR and see what our policies are. I don't want to talk with my manager yet, but maybe I'll need to sooner than I think. Hmmm...

Coach: Sounds like you may have another action...

Gina: Yes. Hey, what am I afraid of? My manager and I get along great. I'm not quitting! I think he'll be thrilled that I'm looking for ways to keep working here.

Coach: Great. And, with that awareness, your actions are....

Gina: First, I want to talk again with my husband and let him know what we've talked about. Then I want to check with HR to see about telecommuting. I want to find out who else is doing it in our company. Maybe HR can tell me. And, I'll start thinking about how to present this to my manager.

Coach: Wow, that's great. By when do you expect to have all these conversations?

Gina: Two weeks, max. I'm ready to go!

The Hourglass Model gives simple structure to the coaching conversation. Part of the value in the Hourglass Model is the strong visual it represents. The next model provides more structure and content to the coaching conversation.

Think about It:

✦ What do you like about the Hourglass Model?

✦ Which part of the model do you think will come most naturally for you? Which will be most difficult? How can you address that difficulty?

✦ What steps can you take to ensure that Jesus is an intimate partner in this coaching model?

✦ Which of the eight coaching skills would be particularly helpful in this model?

The Collaborative Conversation Model

Christian coaches Jeannine Sandstrom and Lee Smith created the Collaborative Conversation Model[2] several years ago. Since then, it has been widely used within organizations. The model was designed to provide structure for coaching conversations, to create a systematic progression toward outcomes, and to encourage collaboration and intentionality when coaching.

Collaborative Conversation Model™

Step 1: Establish Focus

Clarity of focus is critical in coaching. It is important to be specific about the focus—including the intended outcomes, objectives, or goals for the coaching conversation. The wise coach knows what questions to ask the person being coached to clarify the focus as quickly as possible.

Questions to clarify focus include:

- What, specifically, would you like to discuss today?
- What outcomes do you want from this conversation?
- What do you need today from this conversation?

When coaching, it is vital to be clear about what is being discussed. The wise coach takes time to help the person being coached determine what the best focus is and what the desired outcomes are early in the conversation.

---

[2] The model by Lee Smith and Jeannine Sandstrom is available for viewing at www.CoachWorks.com.

Step 2: Discover Possibilities

Once the goals and outcomes are clarified, the next step is to discover possibilities. The coach asks questions to deepen awareness and understanding around the goals and to identify options to move forward.

Questions that promote discovery include:

- What have you already tried that can inform you how to move forward?
- What options are you considering?
- What else?
- What do you know has worked for others?
- As you think about that approach, what outcomes do you anticipate?
- What positive or negative impact needs to be considered?

As the person being coached responds to the questions and explores options and consequences, the coach listens without judging. Listening includes paraphrasing to confirm understanding, exploring consequences, and briefly sharing personal experiences to make pertinent points.

Step 3: Plan the Action

At this point, the coach and the person being coached are clear about the goals for the conversation and have new insight and information that pertain to the goals. The person being coached is ready to develop an action plan. If the goal or task is a big one, it may need to be divided into smaller units that can be managed more easily.

Questions that help to develop an action plan include:

- What actions are you considering that will move you forward?
- What else?
- Considering what's currently on your plate, how reasonable is it for you to meet the deadlines you've identified?
- How can you "chunk" this down?
- Who else needs to be involved with this project?
- What other resources do you need?
- By when do you think you'll complete...?

As you continue to explore actions, be sure that they are aligned with the established focus. Check in often to determine if the actions are practical and reasonable. Be sure to ask about timelines for actions to be taken.

Step 4: Remove Barriers

Anticipating obstacles and thinking about how to overcome them help prepare and empower the person being coached. Surprises will always pop up. It is to everyone's advantage to anticipate and plan for obstacles.

Questions that uncover barriers include:

- What might prevent you from getting the job done?
- Who else needs to be included in this project?
- What will you do if you encounter obstacles?

When discussing this part of the model, be sure to listen to the Holy Spirit. Sometimes the objective coach becomes aware of an obstacle or barrier. Be willing to mention it or ask about something specific that you sense could be a barrier. This is a way of serving the person being coached.

Step 5: Review

One of the biggest mistakes that coaches make at the end of a coaching conversation is not reviewing what has been discussed. To be most effective, invite the person being coached to do the review. When the review is done by the person being coached, the likelihood of commitment and buy-in is greatly increased.

During the recap, the wise coach encourages the person being coached by acknowledging the thinking and/or actions that will be taken. This is also a good time to discuss next steps and to schedule a follow-up coaching call.

Sample questions that encourage a strong recap:

- What was most relevant in this conversation?
- What actions will you take between now and the next time we meet?
- What do you still need to do the project?
- How realistic is the deadline, given your other commitments?
- When would you like to talk again?

Remember Gina from the Hourglass Model? Let's continue the conversation:

Coach: Thanks for calling right on time, Gina. Where would you like to start today?

Gina: I've done a lot since our last call. Talked with HR, and I can telecommute! That's such good news. Gene and I have already looked for houses and found a great one about thirty minutes from his work. That means I can easily get in to my work when needed. I'm actually getting excited!

Coach: You sound excited, Gina! What's most pressing for you right now?

Gina: I need to figure out what I want to do with the worship team. I love being a part, but I don't know if it's realistic.

Coach: In thinking about the worship team, knowing that you really love it, what options do you have?

Gina: I'll definitely need to let our pastor know what's happening, and the worship leader. They need to know what's going on. Soon.

Coach: What are your options with worship?

Gina: They will want me to be there both services. Maybe I could ask to just be part of the late service.

Coach: What else?

Gina: Maybe I could be part of the team once a month rather than weekly? That would maintain the connection and allow us to find a new church that's closer to where we'll be living. Hmmm...

Coach: Great...so now you have three options: Continue with two services each week, ask about being part of the team just one service each week, or ask about being there once a month. What action can you take knowing that you have some options?

Gina: First, I want to talk with Gene to see what he thinks of these ideas. He thought we'd just leave the church, but I'm not sure yet.

Coach: So, you have a fourth option, which is leaving the church, finding a new church, and hopefully a new worship team that's closer to home.

Gina: I think the best option is to see if I can come in once a month for a few months as we look for other churches. I really want to talk with Gene about this.

Coach: What might get in your way of that conversation?

Gina: The kids have so much going on that we don't have much time together without a lot of interference. And, we're so tired at night. Both of us.

Coach: What can you do to create some time for this? It seems pretty important.

Gina: I need to let Gene know that I've got an idea about the move to talk about with him. If he knows it's about the move, he'll want to hear it, so that will help us both to remember.

Coach: And your pastor and worship leader?

Gina: Oh, yes, I'll call tomorrow to set up a time for next week with both of them. That will give Gene and me time to get settled on what we want.

Coach: Great! It's about time to end, so let's quickly review what you'll be doing after we end today. Go ahead...

Gina: I'll talk with Gene tonight. I love the idea we just came up with. Based on what we decide, we'll talk with our pastor and the worship leader by the end of the month. That's two weeks, which should be enough time.

Coach: Wonderful. It will be very fun to hear what comes of these conversations when we next meet.

The power of the Collaborative Conversation Model is that it encourages people to think about what they want to accomplish and to determine how serious they are about moving forward. By asking precise questions, the person being coached discovers more about the goal or project in order to identify actions that are best suited to what's being discussed. Addressing barriers helps to anticipate obstacles that might block progress. Encouraging a strong recap by the person being coached ensures buy-in and commitment to moving forward.

Think about It:

+ What do you like about the Collaborative Conversation Model?

+ Which part of the model do you think will come most naturally for you? Which will be most difficult? How can you address that difficulty?

+ What steps can you take to ensure that Jesus is an intimate partner in this coaching model?

+ Which of the eight coaching skills would be particularly helpful in this model?

Mental Road Map Model

The Mental Road Map Model, developed by Gary Collins,[3] centers on a relationship with Jesus Christ. Every aspect of the coaching relationship relates to Jesus. With Jesus at the core and with a strong coaching relationship, Collins has suggested six main areas to address. These areas can be addressed in any order throughout the coaching relationship. Not all of them will be discussed in any given coaching session. The two main areas to include in most coaching sessions are issues and action.

Issues

Finding the best focus is a central part of coaching. The wise coach begins each coaching call with specific questions that help clarify the focus and the issues for the conversation. This may take several questions, including the sample questions below.

- What exactly does the person being coached want to discuss?
- What are the critical areas that need to be addressed?
- Specifically, what does the person being coached want to gain from the coaching?

---

[3]Gary Collins, *Christian Coaching* (Colorado Springs: NavPress, 2001), 66.

Awareness

A keen awareness of motivation, passion, and values is critical for effective coaching. Awareness was an amazing strength of Jesus. He met people where they were and helped them see where they could be with Him. His encounters with the rich young ruler (Mt. 19:16–24), the woman at the well (Jn. 4:1–42), and Nicodemus (Jn. 3:1–21) are evidence of His awareness as He talked with each of these people. The coach seeks to determine:

- What motivates the person being coached?
- What are the core values of the person being coached, and how do these values impact the focus of the coaching?
- What other areas need to be discussed for the person being coached to move forward effectively?

Vision

Becoming clear about the future is important in coaching. The Scriptures admonish, "Where there is no vision, the people perish" (Prov. 29:18, KJV). Coaching helps individuals find their God-given visions. The coach must help the person determine:

- Where is God leading the person being coached in five years? ten years?
- What vision has the Lord given the person being coached that needs to be considered?
- How can the person being coached discover God's vision?
- What can the person being coached focus on today to move toward the personal vision?

Strategy

Discussing goals is an important part of coaching, especially as they come together toward a desired outcome or end result. A strategy is often put in place to ensure that the end result or outcome is met. Strategies include timelines, resources, and action steps, especially as they relate to specific goals. The best goals are SMART goals (Specific, Measurable, Attainable, Realistic, within a Time frame). Developing strategy requires the person being coached to find out:

- What's the big picture?
- What are the long-term goals?
- What is needed to assist the person being coached in attaining the goals?
- What milestones or targets will ensure reaching the goals?

Action

Thinking about doing something is very different from taking action. Coaching is all about helping people take intentional action. The coach must help find answers to these questions:

- What specific actions is the person being coached willing to take?
- What impact will these actions have on the goals?
- By what specific date will the actions be taken?

Obstacles

Anticipating obstacles, either internal or external, is a great step in overcoming them. The coach is aware that certain questions must be asked:

- What attitudes or thoughts might get in the way of actions and goals?
- What external challenges might get in the way?
- What specifically can the person being coached do to overcome these?

The Mental Road Map Model is unique because Jesus Christ is at the core. Relying on God's presence while listening to the Lord and to the person being coached makes that coaching distinctly Christ-centered.

■ ■ ■ Jose introduced himself to Ron at the coffee shop after noticing Ron reading a novel that Jose himself had recently started. Over the coming weeks they frequently chatted at the coffee shop and found they had a lot in common. One day, Ron seemed unusually distracted, and Jose decided to take a risk and ask him about it.

Jose: Are you okay? You don't seem yourself.

Ron: Sorry, it's just that I have a lot on my mind and some big decisions to make. It seems I'm constantly distracted by all of it. You're not the first to notice.

Jose: You mention some big decisions. If you're comfortable talking about it, so am I.

Ron: Thanks. That would be good. I've been talking to myself about it long enough; maybe it would help to talk with someone else for a change.

Jose: In just a few words, what are the big decisions about? *(Jose decides not to use the word* coach *in a formal way and rather to engage in an informal coaching conversation.)*

Ron: It's about whether or not I should pursue a new job. *(Issues)*

Jose: What makes this decision complicated?

Ron: There are just so many factors involved. There's the money, what a move would do to my family, whether I could do the new job, whether I want to stay stuck in my current job…See, it's complicated. There's just so much to consider.

Jose: You're right, you have many complex issues to consider. Which one issue would prove the most helpful for making the larger decision?

Ron: Well, I think that would have to be my family. I just don't know if my family can handle the move. We all have our friends here, and we are so rooted in this town. We've lived here for nearly a dozen years. Moving would be hard. (*Awareness*)

Jose: This may seem like kind of a personal question, but from what I've picked up on in our previous conversations, you seem to be somewhat of a spiritual person, right?

Ron: Well, I'm not the person I should be, but I consider myself to be a Christian. Why do you ask?

Jose: You know, we each have a value system that helps us filter through the choices we make. When it comes to, "Moving would be hard," how does your faith in Jesus shed light on that truth?

Ron: Wow. I've prayed about the situation, but I've not really considered Jesus to be a value system. The first thing that comes to my mind is that Jesus left the comfort of His place with the Father to minister here on earth. I think there is a passage in Philippians about that.

Jose: How does that affect you and your decision?

Ron: Deep down, I know that I have an impact to make in this world and that I'm not fully living into my potential in my current job. The real issue is whether I am willing to endure the pain of moving to do what I really feel called to do. (*Vision*)

Jose: Are you?

Ron: That's really the question, isn't it? I don't want to endure the pain, but I really believe that the things in life that are worth doing come with a price. I am willing to pay the price for this move. I really am.

Jose: So what will this mean for you?

Ron: It means I need to take the job offer and make this thing happen. It's really time to get on with my life the way it is meant to be lived. I cannot keep using my family as an excuse for not making this move. It's time to act. (*Action*)

Jose: What's the first action you need to take?

Ron: I am going to talk with my wife and share my thoughts about Jesus leaving the comfort of heaven for the sake of others. And I am going to tell her that I am strongly inclined to take the job, even though it means a move and less money.

Jose: Sounds like a big step. What could get in the way? (*Obstacles*)

Ron: The only thing is that I don't know if she will be familiar with that passage. I think it would be best to ask her to read the passage and for us to talk about it before I share with her the implications I am considering.

Jose: I'm not quite finished with my coffee. What else do you need from this conversation?

Ron: I don't think I need anything more. This has been so helpful. My only question is, "Do you think I am making a good decision?"

Jose: Ron, what I think is that you are one of the few people I know who is asking hard questions and who is willing to put Jesus as the core value in your life. If you live into what Jesus wants for your life, I think you'll tend to make very good decisions. What do you think will be consequences of this decision?

Ron: Well, if it's a Jesus-decision, I guess I can expect there could be some pain associated with it and a whole lot of growth. The right thing to do is never easy.

Jose: Is this the right thing to do?

Ron: It is. ■

Think about It:

✦ What do you like about the Mental Road Map Model?

✦ Which part of the model do you think will come most naturally for you? Which will be most difficult? How can you address that difficulty?

✦ What does it mean to you personally for Jesus to be at the core of a model? What steps can you take to ensure that Jesus is preeminent in your coaching relationships?

✦ Which of the eight coaching skills would be particularly helpful in this model?

Moving Forward with Models

The three models presented in this chapter exemplify what coaching looks like. Each model presents a different way of thinking about coaching. Each model requires a variety of coaching skills to be effective.

Remember, you have access to many coaching models. The wise coach looks for new models to use, knows when to use each model, and is agile enough to move among the models according to the need of the person being coached. The wise coach notices what is working well (or not working!) when using the different models.

Think about It:

✦ Which model captures your attention?

✦ When will you try using it?

✦ Be sure to notice what works and what doesn't as part of the learning process. Then, try another model, and another!

✦ What are the important elements that you need to include in all coaching calls?

✦ How will you bring Jesus Christ into the coaching process?

Prayer

Thank You, Lord, for so much variety in our lives: variety in styles, blessings, challenges, coaching skills, and models. Help us to be Masterful, filled with the Master's skills and discernment, as we work with those You send our way. Give us knowledge and wisdom as we coach. Speak powerfully to us and through us as we serve others in Jesus' name. Amen.

Beyond the Book

1. Pick one model and use it intentionally with at least two people whom you are coaching. Notice what works and what doesn't work.
2. Pick a different model and repeat the process. Begin to learn what works best for those you are coaching and for you.
3. Look for coaching books that contain other models. Notice the similarities and differences. Talk with other coaches and find out what models they use.
4. Try new models on a regular basis to expand your learning.
5. If you were to create your own model, what would it look like?

5

The Coaching Relationship

A tradition before any sporting contest–from the Olympic games to backyard football games–has been a signal to start the event. The blowing of a whistle, the shot of a gun, the utterance of words all give the go-ahead for the athletic experience. The underlying assumption is that all participants are ready and willing to do their parts, to fulfill their roles.

So far, this book has focused on coaching definitions, background, skills, and models. With that foundation, it's time for the whistle to blow; it's time for the coaching relationship to begin. This chapter will address the flow of the coaching conversation, including the coaching interview, the first coaching conversations, some elements to consider as coaching unfolds, and the conclusion of the coaching relationship.

The Initial Interview

The first conversation that a coach has with a prospective person to be coached is vitally important because it determines if the person will move forward into coaching and it sets the tone for the ongoing coaching relationship. "A journey of a thousand miles begins with a single step," is a timeworn adage. The initial interview is the first step in the coaching journey.

Before coaching begins, the potential coaching client has heard something about coaching and has heard enough about a particular coach to initiate contact with that person. In this initial contact, both the person to be coached and the coach will have numerous questions.

During this first interview, the following information might be discussed:

1. Requests for information about coaching
2. Requests for information about the coach

3. Desired focus of coaching
4. Dynamics for a successful coaching relationship
5. Confidentiality[1]
6. Parameters of the specific coaching agreement
7. Administrative details
8. Prayer

Requests for Information about Coaching

Many people who inquire about coaching are not sure what coaching really is and so will ask about it. Be ready to share what coaching is and what to expect within a coaching relationship. Be brief and clear. For example, "Coaching is different from consulting or therapy. Coaching starts with where you are and focuses on where you want to go. It is not about the past or what has transpired to this point. It is always focused on taking intentional action. By the way, most coaching is done by telephone, which saves time and money!" For more information about coaching as distinct from other service professions, see appendix 1, "Distinctions of Coaching," p. 125. Appendix 2, "Sample Coaching Documents" (p. 127), has an informational page on coaching (Sample 9) that could be shared with potential coaching clients.

Requests for Information about the Coach

Coaches might be asked to share about their experience, their "best" clients, their background, their faith story, or even about their family. Be prepared to answer each question without being too wordy. Be brief, then turn the conversation back to the other person by asking a question such as, "What else would you like to know?" or, "What about you...what information do you want to share about yourself?"

In addition, questions may arise about the style of coaching. Think about your own coaching style or personality. Think about what others have said about you to determine your style. For example, some people are direct while others are more indirect. Some look more at strategy or tactics. If you know your style, it can be useful to share it during interviews. For example, you might say, "You may be wondering what kind of style I use when I am coaching. I am sensitive to what's going on under the surface and will be direct in asking you if something is incongruent. How will that work for you?"

---

[1]See International Code of Ethics, www.coachfederation.org: "I will respect the confidentiality of my client's information, except as otherwise authorized by my client, or as required by law. I will obtain agreement from my clients before releasing their names as clients or references, or any other client-identifying information. I will obtain agreement from the person being coached before releasing information to another person compensating me."

Desired Focus of Coaching

Be sure to ask the person the primary reason for seeking to be coached at this time. Ask questions that help the person be as specific as possible, such as, "At the end of three months, what do you hope to be different?" or, "What would a successful outcome look like?" Be sure to let the potential client know that the person being coached, not the coach, sets the agenda for each coaching session. For example, you could say, "You will be determining what we talk about, so at the beginning of each conversation, I will start by asking you what you want to focus on."

Dynamics for a Successful Coaching Relationship

An initial conversation with a potential coaching client should include a discussion about honesty, openness, trust, and safety. The conversation might include, "Successful coaching is based on both of us being honest and open with each other. If either of us sees something that isn't working, let's have permission to share it and to determine how to move forward."

Confidentiality

Be sure to include information about confidentiality in the initial interview. For example, you could simply say, "Our relationship is a confidential one. That means that you can share anything you want, but I won't share anything you have told me with anyone, unless it is reportable by law. So, no one will know we're working together unless you let them know."

Parameters of the Specific Coaching Agreement

Most new clients who want to know about coaching also want to know how coaching works. The following information should be shared during the initial interview:

- How frequently will coaching conversations occur?
- Will coaching conversations be conducted by telephone or in person?
- If by telephone, who will call whom?
- What will be the length of each coaching conversation?
- How long is the initial coaching contract?

After an initial introductory discussion, a coach might say, "I suggest that we contract for three months of coaching by telephone. Since you're in a different city, this will save you time and money. Even though we'll make progress from the start, it usually takes several coaching calls to develop our coaching relationship, so a three-month contract is a good starting place. I suggest two hours of coaching each month, which means two calls of an hour each. I'd like you to call me, and if I haven't heard from you by five minutes after our scheduled time, I will call you. How does that sound to you? (*pause*) During our first call, I'll be asking you what you want to accomplish during our coaching. We can refine this as we go."

You could also add, "If we get into the first three months and determine that it isn't working, we will talk about it and stop if needed. In other words, if we determine that we aren't working well together, then we will end the contract wherever we are."

Administrative Details

All administrative details of the coaching relationship should be clear. The initial conversation should include discussion about calls being on time, a twenty-four–hour cancellation policy, fees, how and when the coach wants to be paid (monthly or quarterly, by check or money order, through PayPal, etc.). For example, the discussion might include, "As we start to work together, I will set aside the time for our calls and will call you if you haven't called within five minutes of the starting time. If you need to cancel, please give me twenty-four hours notice as you would any professional service provider. I will do the same. Our agreed-upon fee is $_____. I prefer to be paid by check each month. If you prefer to pay on a quarterly basis, that's fine, too. Do you have any questions or concerns?" It is often helpful to put the details of the coaching relationship in writing to minimize miscommunication or confusion. See appendix 2, "Sample Coaching Documents" (p. 127), for more information.

Prayer

If the person being coached is a believer, discuss including prayer at the beginning and/or end of each coaching session. For example, you could say, "You've mentioned that you are a believer. Some people like to include prayer at the beginning and at the end of each coaching conversation, and some don't. What's your preference?" Respect the person's preferences. Whether or not you pray aloud with the person being coached, the wise Christian coach always seeks God's presence and guidance prior to and during coaching conversations.

The initial interview is a critical time of connecting while exchanging information. When being interviewed, the coach must be comfortable answering questions and clarifying expectations. It is helpful to take notes during the interview so that they can be referenced when the coaching gets started. Be sure to take notes on the focus of the coaching, the agreements around fees and initial commitments, and contact information. (See appendix 2, "Sample Coaching Documents," p. 127.)

▪ ▪ ▪ As soon as Lira heard about coaching, and particularly about Dee, a local coach, she was intrigued. She called Dee immediately and said, "I am very interested in coaching and have heard about you. Can you tell me a bit about what you do as a coach?"

Dee responded, "Thanks for calling, Lira. As you may know, coaching is all about taking action. It's not counseling–which is about the past and its impact on the present–and it's not consulting. It's all about moving forward. I've been coaching for two years and love seeing the people I work with take action and move from where they are to where they want to be. Can you share a bit about yourself and what you might want to work on?"

Lira said, "My role in our church has just changed. Instead of being part of the worship team, I'm now leading it. I'm a little intimidated by the role and want to get started well."

"How wonderful that your skills and gifts have been recognized! Congratulations. I have a sense that we could start coaching right now, but before that, what other questions do you have?"

Lira thought for a minute, then asked, "What's the process of coaching like?"

Dee responded right away, "Just like this phone call, coaching takes place by phone. Everything we discuss is confidential, which means that you can share about it but I won't, unless there's something that is reportable by law. For a strong coaching relationship, we will want to be honest with each other. If something isn't working, let's talk about it. Usually we meet for two hours a month, which can be thirty minutes each week or an hour every other week. Which would be best for you?"

"An hour every other week will fit well into my schedule. Who calls whom?"

"Great question, Lira. Since we're both here in town, I'll call you when we're scheduled to talk. Like other professional service providers, I like to have twenty-four hours notice if a call needs to be rescheduled or cancelled. Will that work for you?"

"Absolutely, Dee. That's great. Obviously this is a valuable service, so what are your fees?"

"The fee for two hours of coaching per month is $___ per month, which can be paid via check at the beginning of the relationship or monthly. Do you think that will work for you?"

"Yes, that's very fair. How will we know if it's working?"

Dee laughed. "Let's turn that question back to you, Lira. How will you know if it's working?"

"I suppose that if I feel like I'm making progress and that the worship team is working well together, that will let me know it's working."

"What else?"

Lira thought for a moment. "If I feel good about myself as a worship leader and if it's not taking over my life, that will be wonderful. I'm concerned about the amount of time this might take up. I want to have plenty of time for my family and my ministry."

"So now we have several more things to think about as we're coaching: you as a worship leader, determining how much time you want to spend, and being sure you are still focusing on your family. Here's what I would suggest. Based on what you've shared, how about if we start with three months of coaching, with an hour call every other week? If at any time either of us determines that this isn't working, we'll talk about it and be willing to stop. If it's going well, we'll reevaluate how we're doing and if you want to continue after three months. How does that work for you?

"Great. When can we start?" ▪

Think about It:

✦ Which of the various components of the initial interview do you believe is most important?

✦ Practice sharing the information, being sure to include all the components you feel are important, so that you are ready for that first call!

The First Coaching Conversation

At this point, the initial interview has been completed, and the potential client has decided to move forward with coaching. A coaching call has been scheduled. In preparing for this call, remember to pray and relax, to review notes from the initial interview, and to prepare to review with the person being coached some key elements discussed in the interview. During the review, try to take less than five minutes to discuss key agreements. Don't drag this part out!

One way to review the key elements of the interview would be to say:

"Before we start, may I review a few things about how we'll work together?

Just as a reminder, our relationship is confidential. That means that you can share anything you want and you can trust that I won't share that information with anyone else.

"We are going to start with three months of coaching by telephone. We're going to be scheduling two hours of coaching monthly, which means two calls of an hour each. I'd like you to call me, and if I haven't heard from you by five minutes after the hour, I will call you.

"If we get into the first three months and determine that it isn't working, we will talk about it and stop if needed. In other words, if we determine that we aren't working well together, then we will end the contract wherever we are.

"Successful coaching is based on both of us being honest and open with each other. If either of us sees something that isn't working, let's share it and determine how to move forward. If you need to cancel, please give me twenty-four–hours notice as you would any professional service provider. I will do the same.

"Finally, *you* will determine what we talk about, so at the beginning of each call, I will ask you what you want to focus on. Do you have any questions before we begin? Great. Where would you like to start today?"

When the person being coached answers that first question, relax and put into practice the first two core coaching skills: listening and asking precise questions. As a coach grows in coaching skill and experience, the first coaching session will become stronger. At the end of it, be sure to ask the person being coached to identify anything that would make the coaching experience better. Ask what worked and what could be improved. Be open to how the person being coached responds and show flexibility by adjusting what is needed. Above all, keep focused on serving the person as a way of serving the Lord. The apostle Paul said it well, "Serve one another in love" (Gal. 5:13).

As the Conversation Unfolds

When the coaching journey begins, neither the coach nor the person being coached truly knows where the journey will take them. What is known is that good coaching always focuses on the person being coached.

■ ■ ■ When Diana started receiving coaching, she had no idea that it would change her life. She had been ready to leave her company after being recruited by another company. During the first coaching conversation, Diana shared her dilemma.

"How is God leading you?" asked her coach, knowing that Diana was a believer.

"I'm not sure. I don't sense a peace about leaving yet."

"What do you really want?"

Diana replied, "If I could figure out a way to stay and get compensated in a way that works, that's what I want."

"It's time to ask for what you want!" responded her coach immediately. (*The coach delivered a direct message.*)

Four years later, Diana continues to be one of the top sales people at the same company. She is widely respected, is sought out as a thought leader, and is compensated well. She knows she is in the center of God's will. ■

Understanding the Dynamics of Coaching Conversations

Concepts Relevant to Coaching

Coaching conversations are simple, yet complex and multifaceted. They promote discovery as they encourage people to take intentional action. Bacon and Spear[2] offer the following conversation concepts relevant to coaching:

- The purpose is to facilitate open communication.
- Participants should be unbiased and open to exploration.
- One key goal is not to engage in a debate, where there are winners and losers. In coaching, everyone wins.
- Another goal is to understand how hidden values and intentions control behavior so that appropriate action is taken.
- There is no single right answer. There may be multiple "truths" from multiple perspectives.
- Two primary skills are asking and listening.
- Participants must learn to suspend judgment. Fault-finding is anathema to the process.
- Participants do not necessarily have to agree with one another. The goal is not to reach consensus, though that may be an outcome. The goal is intentional action.
- As trust grows, so does the participant's willingness to disclose thoughts and feelings that are usually hidden, which results in greater insight, leading to more effective action.

Think about It: ————————————————————————

✦ Which of these concepts do you believe will be the most challenging for you personally as a coach?

✦ What specific steps can you take to address that challenge?

God's Part in Coaching

Coaching is a collaborative exploration focusing on the person being coached and producing discovery at many levels. The role of the coach is critical in the exploration process. In Christian coaching, God's role through the Holy Spirit is the most important element.

As depicted in the diagram on page 76, God is a part of all coaching conversations with believers. His presence impacts discussions, as each person experiences God's nudges and discusses what is being experienced.

---

[2]Terry Bacon and Karen Spear, *Adaptive Coaching* (Palo Alto, Calif.: Davies-Black, 2003), 136–37.

Coaching can address and strengthen each person's relationship with God as well as focus on what the person being coached wants to discuss.

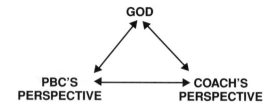

As the root of the Christian Coaching Relationship Tree from chapter 1 (see p. 11) demonstrates, Christian coaching is based on the belief that God is intimately involved in the coaching relationship. With the Lord's help, the person being coached can access answers. Therefore, it is *not* the role of the coach to find solutions. It *is* the role of the coach to listen and encourage the person being coached into expanded thinking and solutions, relying on the Holy Spirit's leadership. The coach is not the one who has to solve the situation. The coach sends a powerful message by believing that the person being coached, with the assistance of the Holy Spirit, has the answers and by staying in a listening mode long enough for the person being coached to discover those answers and solutions.

Theologian R. C. Sproul once wrote,

> He is intangible and invisible. But His work is more powerful than the most ferocious wind. The Spirit brings order out of chaos and beauty out of ugliness. He can transform a sin-blistered man into a paragon of virtue. The Spirit changes people. The Author of life is also the Transformer of life.[3]

The Holy Spirit is a vital participant in the Christian coaching relationship! The Christian coach brings a strong belief that the person being coached, with the help of the Holy Spirit, can discover the solutions that will move that person forward.

When the Person Has No Solutions

But what happens when the person being coached really does not have the solutions? Here are three helpful reminders:

- Coaching does not anticipate that persons being coached will discover technical or specialized knowledge. For example, coaching will not help a person discover how to play the guitar, perform surgery, or fill out taxes.

---

[3]R. C. Sproul, *The Mystery of the Holy Spirit* (Wheaton, Ill.: Tyndale House, 1994), 7.

- Coaching can often help the person being coached discover a specific learning gap and identify how best to fill the gap. For example, Rich is a pastor who realized through coaching that he knew very little about staff development and that this gap was constantly creating challenges for him. Coaching helped him identify a trusted mentor with an excellent track record of developing strong staff teams. Rich determined that this mentor could get him started in learning what he needed to know.
- Coaching can help a person being coached commit to learning what needs to be learned. Many coaching actions involve the person being coached learning from an external source. Action identification and negotiation helps the client discover the right action and take that action, especially when the action involves closing a skill or knowledge gap.

Attitudes, Biases, Judgments, Beliefs

For coaching to work well, the coach must be aware of personal attitudes, biases, judgments, and beliefs. These impact behaviors, whether consciously or not. The wise coach knows his or her own biases or judgments so that they don't impact the coaching relationship negatively. This seems easy, but isn't. So many different subjects can be brought into the coaching conversation! Think about how beliefs can impact behavior.

The Coach's Beliefs Impact Behavior

What if a bias or a negative attitude or judgment is affecting the coaching relationship?

- Own it! "I realize that I have a bias around what we're discussing. May I share it with you so it's on the table and so that it doesn't get in the way?" Or, "I just realized that my last comment is more about me than it is about you. My attitude just got in the way. I'm really sorry. Let's try that again."
- Take responsibility for it. "I am feeling strongly about what's being discussed. This is about me, not you. I take responsibility for my feelings and will try to stay focused on you."
- Ask for help. "I know that this is a hot topic for me. If you sense that my attitude is getting in the way, please call me on it!"

Think about It —————————————————————————————

✦ What is your attitude toward women who are senior pastors?

✦ What do you think about people who dislike being part of a team?

✦ What are your beliefs about abortion?

✦ What do you believe about people who make decisions more slowly than you? Or more quickly?

✦ What do you think about motorcycle riders?

✦ What are your thoughts about the postmodern generation?

✦ What is your attitude toward those who raise their hands during worship? toward those who don't?

✦ How will you handle your own biases and attitudes when they begin to show up in coaching conversations?

✦ Are there other "hot-button" topics for you that you can anticipate? How will you address those situations if they arise?

Depending on how strongly you believe, and depending on what the person being coached shares with you, situations may lead you to suggest a referral to another coach. Be prepared to do this if you believe that personal beliefs or attitudes might cloud the coaching.

Understanding Personality and Style

Understanding people, including their personalities and styles, is useful when coaching. This includes knowing your own personality and style as well as understanding others'. Part of the coach's role is to adapt to others' styles and use effective language that resonates with the person being coached. Much information on style and personality is in the marketplace. All of these help inform coaches about their clients. For a partial list of resources in this area, see appendix 5, "Resources for Coaching" (p. 145).

As you coach, you gain more knowledge about yourself and the person you're coaching. You will need to consider many aspects, both in terms of self-knowledge and growth as well as knowledge about the person you're coaching. Some of these are depicted in the tree diagram in chapter 1 (see p. 11.) The roots of the Christian coaching relationship are in Christ, with both the coach and person being coached bringing their unique gifts and personalities to the relationship. In the ideal relationship, the personalities mesh, and the branches of the coaching tree expand in discovery and action.

Sometimes a personality mismatch occurs. When that happens, the wise coach will address it directly with the person being coached in a straightforward and nonjudgmental way. Several outcomes may occur. The person being coached may not think a problem exists. At this point, the coach needs to decide if coaching can continue. The person being coached might agree that something isn't working, and then a referral may be needed.

In this case, a wise coach is willing to offer the best referral possible. Occasionally, just by addressing the situation directly, the coach and person being coached can re-contract and move forward. If this is the outcome, check in frequently or determine the process for evaluating the relationship, to be sure that the coaching relationship is working for the person being coached. If not, be willing to provide a referral.

Nurturing the Coaching Relationship

Sometimes a coaching relationship will continue for a number of months or even longer. As the relationship continues and grows, the coach can affirm the person being coached and nurture the relationship by simple, thoughtful gestures. Consider the following ideas:

- Send birthday and holiday cards.
- Never withhold anything from the person being coached. Always share everything with the person being coached, including your concerns or fears about the individual or situation, or how that person is being perceived. Be honest.
- Under-promise always. Never even hint that you can produce miracles.
- Don't get into personality issues; keep the coaching focused on actions.
- Acknowledge goals met on behalf of the person being coached. Make a congratulatory phone call or send a congratulatory e-mail or handwritten note.
- Speak with the person being coached between calls occasionally. Assure the person of your prayers.
- Consider inviting persons being coached and their friends to social events or special workshops.
- Send out a quarterly letter or newsletter of useful information.
- Get the person being coached to focus on a big and exciting goal or project. Challenge, but don't coddle, the person.[4]

Recognizing Holy Nudges

As you coach, be aware of what's happening in the coaching conversation. Begin to recognize and respond to subtle ideas, thoughts, or nudges. Consider these as proddings from the Holy Spirit. They may be about tone, pace, mismatch of style, level of directness, biases, or a myriad of other things. God's gentle nudges can produce profound responses. "Since we live by the Spirit, let us keep in step with the Spirit" (Gal. 5:25).

■ ■ ■ Mary heard about coaching and called Ed, a coach to whom she had been referred. When she and Ed had their first interview, Mary was impressed.

[4]Copyright © 2005 by Coach U. Inc., from www.coachu.com.

Toward the interview's end, Ed, a relatively new coach, felt a nudge to ask several questions that he didn't normally ask. One question in particular was one that Ed had never asked before. "Mary, how was the pace?" Mary laughed out loud as she replied matter-of-factly, "I...love...the...conversation...we've...just...had, ...but...if...you...don't... slow... down,... I... won't... be... able ...to... keep... up... with... you."

Ed laughed with Mary. He knew he'd been nudged by the Holy Spirit and had asked the right question. He responded, "It is my responsibility to match my pace to yours. If either of us feels like I am going too fast, we'll bring it up and talk about it." Mary and Ed worked together for more than a year, and it was largely due to Ed's willingness to respond to nudges from the Holy Spirit.■

Closing the Coaching Relationship

Every coaching relationship that begins will end at some point. It may end quickly or may take years before drawing to a close. Regardless of when the coaching relationship ends, you need to remember some points.

1. Take time to end the coaching well. The wise coach knows what to include so that the person being coached is well taken care of at the end of the coaching relationship.

2. Let the person being coached know when the end of the coaching contract is approaching. If the coaching contract called for six coaching sessions over a three-month period, begin talking about closing down the conversations by the fifth session. One way to say this would be, "Today is the fifth of six coaching calls that we agreed to when we started. I wanted to remind you so that we can be sure to focus on the things that are most important to you. Next time we talk, since it will be our last call, I would like us to set aside at least fifteen minutes to get good closure on the work you've done. Would that be okay with you? Now, where would you like to focus today?"

3. Be prepared for the person being coached to ask for an extension of the coaching. Don't expect this to happen all the time; yet, be prepared when it does. Then, take the time to draw out the objectives from the person being coached for continuing the coaching. Then re-contract for the additional time.

4. Know what to include for good closure. To gain good closure, be sure to say anything that needs to be said, to take time for both the person being coached and the coach to share their experiences of what has occurred over the course of the coaching, to acknowledge the person being coached for the work that has been done and the actions taken, to encourage the person being coached to continue moving forward,

and to be sure that the door is left open for later contact if desired by the person being coached.

5. Express interest in what's ahead for the person being coached. In some instances where a strong and healthy relationship has developed, it can be appropriate for the coach to invite the person being coached to stay in touch. This is encouraging to the person being coached and is a way of acknowledging the relationship.

The coaching relationship is unique both for the coach and for the person being coached. The wise coach knows the value of each part of the coaching relationship: the initial interview, the first coaching session, the unfolding coaching conversation, and ending well. The wise coach knows how to step firmly into each part and to create value for the person being coached.

Prayer

Lord, we acknowledge Your presence as we get started with each coaching client. Help us be aware that we are serving You in all our conversations. Nudge us when You want us to notice something or when we are insensitive so that we can be used mightily by You in others' lives. Teach us about ourselves as we interact with others. Show us how to honor You as we end the coaching relationships that You bring our way. In all our relationships, help us to recognize Your voice and to obey Your leading so that You are glorified. In Jesus' name, Amen.

Beyond the Book

1. What do you need to do to be ready for people to call and interview you?
2. How can you get firsthand experience in the interviewing process to see how others handle this important part of the coaching relationship?
3. What do you need to know, to get, or to do to be ready for your first coaching conversations?
4. What questions can you ask to help the person being coached get focused at the beginning of each call?
5. What elements do you want to include in the final coaching session?
6. How can you deepen your roots in Christ throughout the coaching relationship?
7. What does God want you to recognize about yourself that will help you become a wise coach?

6

A Coach Approach to
Ministry Leadership

■ ■ ■ "But I am not paid to coach, I am paid to lead."

The voice came from the back of the room about an hour into a three-day coaching workshop. All eyes turned to the source of the comment: John, a senior manager within a large private hospital in the Midwest. John continued, "And leading means telling people what to do, not asking them what they want to do." ■

Many coach training experiences—be it in the church or the corporate arena—include some variant of John's comment. Pastors, managers, denominational ministers, executives, and even front-line supervisors wrestle with how to integrate coaching into their leadership functions. They wonder and sometimes verbalize the question: "What is a coach approach to leadership?"

Perhaps the last thing ministry leaders need is new leadership advice. Many ministry leaders have shelves that buckle beneath the advice, encouragement, and admonishment of those who purport to know how others ought to lead.

The deluge of leadership "wisdom" in the past decades points to two realities. First, many people are now confused about how to lead. Should leaders lead like the great warriors Sun Tzu and Robert E. Lee, or be a CEO like Jesus? Should leaders offer leadership and act as servants, or have a "take no prisoners" mentality? Everyone from overpaid and under-performing executives to ivory tower elites have contributed to the cacophony of what it means to lead. The whole mess can get quite confusing.

Second, would-be leaders need help. The irony is that leadership books continue to be on best-selling lists and create this leadership labyrinth because of the real need to understand leadership.

This chapter will discuss the role of the leader in light of coaching. Coaching is not synonymous with leadership. However, a good leader can use a coach approach to lead more effectively.

Leadership?

What is leadership? How have you heard others define it? What is your own working definition? One favorite leadership proverb sets the tone for true leadership: "The one who says he is a leader and has no followers is merely taking a walk."

Quite simply, a leader is someone with followers. In an even smaller nutshell, leadership is influence. The leader influences others toward a new reality. Good leadership is about influencing others forward toward a better reality. Ken Blanchard teaches that leadership is an influence process in which leaders work with people to help them accomplish their goals and the goals of the organization.

Since leadership is influence, the scope of who is a leader is wide open. Leaders are not merely, or even primarily, high-flying executives or renowned people of power. Almost every individual extends influence with peers, family, organizations, and even self. A good leader takes seriously the opportunity to influence and is somewhat intentional about exercising that influence toward outcomes, such as a strong family, profitable business, missional church, or litter-free neighborhood.

The Leader Takes Responsibility with Humility

Jim Collins describes the "Level Five Leader" through a metaphor that involves a window and a mirror. The Level Five Leader, when things are going well, looks out the window and assigns credit to someone or something outside of self, such as followers, context, a lucky break, or even a competitor's mishap. When things are going badly, the Level Five Leader looks in the mirror and takes responsibility. By contrast, the poor leader reverses the metaphor, looking in the mirror (taking credit) for things that go well and looking outside the window (blaming others) when things go badly. Collins believes that these contrasting perspectives have nothing to do with reality. That is, the Level Five Leader did help create good outcomes and had no control over potential misfortunes. The perspective is important. Perspective combines responsibility with humility, or as Collins puts it: Professional Will and Personal Humility.[1]

---

[1]Jim Collins, *From Good to Great: Why Some Companies Make the Leap...and Others Don't* (New York: HarperCollins, 2001), 36.

The Two Sides of Level 5 Leadership[2]

Professional Will	Personal Humility
Creates superb results, a clear catalyst in the transition from good to great.	Demonstrates a compelling modesty, shunning public adulation, never boastful.
Demonstrates an unwavering resolve to do whatever must be done to produce the best long-term results, no matter how difficult.	Acts with quiet, calm determination; relies principally on inspired standards, not inspiring charisma, to motivate.
Sets the standard of building an enduring great company; will settle for nothing less.	Channels ambition into the company, not the self; sets up successors for even greater success in the next generation.
Looks in the mirror, not out the window, to apportion responsibility for poor results, never blaming other people, external factors, or bad luck.	Looks out the window, not in the mirror, to apportion credit for the success of the company – to other people, external factors, and good luck.

Coaching as a Third Alternative to Leadership Options

So where does coaching fit into leadership? Coaching can navigate a healthy course between two bad options for leaders. Like the Greek mythological hero Odysseus sailing between Scylla and Charybdis, the leader must avoid two dreadfully destructive and inflexible options.

First, the leader must avoid the "command and demand" option. This leadership style involves the heavy-handed person who barks orders and creates tension among followers to get results. This is the "my way or the highway" leader, the micromanager who wants everything a specific way and on an unreasonable timetable. This is the "if I want your opinion, I'll give it to you" boss. Of course, these descriptions paint a dramatic caricature, but many leaders do display this sort of inflexible style. They have gone off the deep end of responsibility and authority and have excluded everyone else from the leadership equation. The results of this style often include: low buy-in, reluctant followers, tension, less-than-best decisions because of the myopic nature of the decision-making process, and lack of effective leadership succession since the leader never shares the leadership role.

Second, the leader must avoid the "refrain and abstain" option. This leadership style abdicates too much responsibility to followers. It is a *laissez-faire* approach that takes empowerment too far and results in a hands-off reality that leaves too much to the initiative of followers. In an attempt to democratize the leadership role, this option leaves everyone wondering, "Who is the leader?" This option often produces results such as chaos, lack of a guiding and unifying vision, competing realities offered from those

---

[2]Ibid.

who wish to fill the leadership vacuum, and followers who are unmotivated because of lack of contact from the leader.

Two Inflexible and Destructive Leadership Options

Inflexible Option	"Command and Demand"	"Refrain and Abstain"
Typified By	• Authoritarian • Nothing is outside the leader's direct influence • Exclusion of others from decision-making	• Abdication of duty • Little contact between leader and little influence • "Who is leading?"
Results in	• Low buy-in • Reluctant or fearful followers • Tension • Less-than-best decisions made without full resources of the team • Poor leadership succession	• Chaos • No guiding or unifying vision • Competing realities • Leadership vacuum • Delayed decisions • Lack of motivation

Bringing Out Self-leadership

Coaching enables the leader to be flexible, to adjust to the needs of the context, and to bring out the best of the two inflexible options while avoiding the dangers inherent in each. Coaching navigates between the rocks of inflexibility by giving the leader skills for including others while maintaining a powerful and influential presence. It truly enables the leader to tap into "the best of both worlds."

This is not to say that coaching equals leadership. In its purest form, coaching is a relationship that accentuates the client's own self-leadership. The person being coached brings the agenda, develops fresh insights, and gains commitment to new and better actions. The coach is not the key influencer in the relationship. Rather, the coach plays a supporting role in bringing out the best self-leadership from the client.

While coaching is not exclusively equated with leadership, a leader's style and practice should have a place for coaching. This is "a coach approach to leadership."

Coaching in a Leader's Life

Coaching gets played out in the life of a leader in two distinct ways.

The first coach approach to leadership is direct coaching. That is, sometimes a leader may need to coach a follower in a pure and straightforward way. In such instances the leader will act more like a coach than like any other role, such as consultant, counselor, mentor, director, or trainer. For more information about coaching as distinct from other service professions, see appendix 1, "Distinctions of Coaching" (p. 125). Coaching works best when the follower has some competence for a task or decision but lacks confidence and/or commitment. In these cases, the leader will want to coach the follower to uncover that person's ability to succeed. This could be a short-term coaching relationship or an interaction that lasts several months. The key is that the leader knows coaching to be the best way to help the follower move forward, get to what is next, and develop into an even bigger contributor—one who brings competence, confidence, and commitment. If the follower has little or no competence, more direction would be needed at first before using a coach approach.

■ ■ ■ Jackson is a worship leader who reports directly to the senior pastor, Bob, who is head of staff for the mid-size congregation. Jackson is a superior worship leader for the congregation's liturgical Sunday morning services, but he is faced with what to do with a Sunday night praise service that he feels inadequate to lead. He asked the pastor, "What should I do?"

Pastor Bob explained that he was in no position to tell Jackson what to do, since Jackson was the real expert in this situation. Instead, he offered to coach Jackson. Having given a brief description of coaching, Pastor Bob took a coach approach and began exploring the landscape of the situation with Jackson. Without offering advice or direction, Pastor Bob helped Jackson highlight what issues were involved and helped Jackson to articulate clearly some possible options, including:

1. Continue "as is" and learn to deal with the anxiety and less-than-best results.
2. Find someone passionate and gifted with the praise service and give leadership of the praise service to that person.
3. Find someone passionate and gifted with the praise service and manage that person's leadership of the service.
4. Transform the Sunday evening service into something that more closely fits Jackson's abilities and passions.
5. Discontinue the praise service, since it does not fit Jackson's skill set and passion.
6. Resign so the congregation can find someone equally gifted for liturgical and praise worship services.

Once the options were listed and explored, Pastor Bob asked Jackson which of the options were not really options, after all. Jackson responded by crossing off options 1, 4 and 5, since option 1 didn't solve anything and options 4 and 5 seemed to place Jackson above the needs of the congregation. Pastor Bob then shifted from coach to leader and told Jackson that he would not allow for option 6 because Jackson was a valuable part of the body and he did not want to lose him. With the landscape of options getting clearer, Pastor Bob coached Jackson to further explore options 2 and 3 by establishing some guidelines for determining which option was the best. Jackson determined that his integrity would not allow him simply to "shove the responsibility off to someone else." This left option 3. Jackson committed to exercising responsibility for the service by managing someone whose gifts and passion were more closely aligned with the praise service. ∎

A second coach approach to leadership is perhaps more common: a leader may use some of the skills and practices of coaching in the everyday leadership role. While not pure coaching, this approach to leadership and coaching brings in many of the benefits of coaching to the aspects of the leader's role. To help flesh out a coach approach to ministry leadership, consider three common aspects of leadership for a ministry leader: vision caster, manager, and shepherd.

The triple roles of vision caster, manager, and shepherd relate to a commonly accepted understanding of what it means to be a pastor. These roles mirror the offices of Christ: prophet, king, and priest. Similarly, effective pastors must lead well in each of three aspects: theologically (prophet), organizationally (king), and relationally (priest).[3] Theologically, a pastor must be in touch with the story of what God is up to historically, biblically, and congregationally. As vision caster, the pastor brings theology to bear on a congregation. Organizationally, the effective pastor must lead the congregation as an institution. Like other organizations, a congregation requires plans to be made and executed, and the pastor must manage the processes. Finally, as shepherd, the pastor relates to the persons of the congregation as individuals and as participants in the life of the community. Pastors must relate well to people as they journey.

Coaching can positively impact each of these roles. Though not all leaders fulfill these exact roles, similarities between pastoral leadership and leadership in other ministry contexts provide a variety of opportunities to apply these lessons to other leadership contexts.

Visioning: A Coach Approach to Theological Leadership

Many leaders define their primary role in terms of visioning. They discern the direction for the organization and help others move toward that better future. Indeed, the ability to think forward and imagine what is possible is vitally important for leaders.

---

[3]Dan Allender notes the threefold office of Christ as being parallel to that of pastoral leaders in "The Psychology of a Pooped Pastor," an address at the 2003 Pooped Pastors conference in Orlando, Florida. Allender also parallels these offices to the role of mentors in "Mimicking Our Disruptive Father and Our Diverse Older Brother: Learning Prophetic Disruption, Priestly Connection, and Kingly Service," *1996 Mars Hill Review* (Summer 1996): 34–46.

Some favorite role models for today's leaders are individuals who were uniquely able to see forward and communicate a fresh vision with clarity, passion, and inspiration. Leaders like Mahatma Gandhi (who based much of his leadership on that of Christ), Winston Churchill, Moses, and Clara Barton stand out as figures who led others to live toward the futures they imagined. These and other great leaders are known for their ability to discern and cast vision.

Getting a Vision

But where is this "vision," and how does the leader get it? Three common responses are that God gives vision to the leader, or that the leader "goes to the mountain" and sees the vision in isolation, or that the vision comes to the leader in a dream. Certainly each of these options is a possibility. But the vision caster who takes a coach approach has one more option: the vision may reside with the followers.

Ministry leaders, especially those in faith families who value the priesthood of all believers, possess a theological impetus for believing that vision resides with the community. In such cases, the vision caster is charged, not with coming up with the vision in solitude, but with discerning the vision from amidst the community. This could be termed "skimming for the vision." The picture is that various members of a church (or any organization) have a piece of the vision. Through experience, intellect, relationships, and ability, each of these members carries God-given hopes, dreams, concerns, and suggestions for the church. The vision caster who dialogues with members uses the skills of a coach to draw out the vision from each person. The vision caster asks questions, listens intently, suspends judgment, and even encourages forward movement in an effort to support the "persons being coached" while simultaneously picking up one more aspect of God's intent for the church.

Skimming for the vision is not an abdication of the leader's duty to discern vision. This is not "vision by committee." Instead, skimming for the vision is a way to discern. The leader must have eyes to see and ears to hear the vision as it is revealed piece by piece. Talk about active listening! The leader must distinguish what is and what is not a piece of the vision, hold onto each piece as it is revealed, prayerfully recognize patterns and themes that emerge, and then put these pieces together with God's help. Skimming for the vision is not a shortcut to discerning the vision for a church, but it is a way of tapping into the genius of the community. A leader's decision to take an initiative or recommend an action comes from that leader's intuition, experience, and intelligence. A coach approach enables the leader to tap into the intuition, experience, and intelligence of many people.

When the leader moves from discerning vision to casting vision, the hard coaching work that goes into skimming for the vision pays off. A repeated benefit of coaching is that people are committed to that for which they feel ownership. A wise leader is able to communicate how the vision emerged and how community members contributed to the discernment process. Again, many coaching skills go into this. The leader will use various forms of responding to help each member of the congregation recognize the vision as his or her own. The congregational leader will say, "This is what I heard you say." The "you" carries a double meaning of both multiple singulars and one plural.

By using coaching skills, a leader can also be more effective in helping people realize the vision that has been discerned. This is an aspect of casting whereby the leader coaches individuals or teams to envision their own futures in light of the congregation's unifying vision. A leader might ask powerful coaching questions such as:

- "Based on what's next for the church, what might be next for this ministry?"
- "What details are already in sharp focus, and which need further clarification?"
- "In addition to prayer, how might this team go about discerning the unique way our common vision will be made real in this ministry?"
- "What's your next action, and where does it lead?"

Think about It:

✦ Think of one or two additional questions you might add to the list above for individuals or teams in the church.

A vision discerned in community and cast in community will likely be owned by community. Again, this is not "vision by committee." The leader is still responsible for vision. Even with a coach approach, the leader maintains the unique and significant role of being the one who discerns and casts the vision. By taking a coach approach, the leader goes about discerning and casting in a more curious and communal way.

▪ ▪ ▪ Consider the experience of Pastor Dave, who had been pressured to resign after two years at this church. When he signed up for a coach-training program, he wanted to consider "what might be next for a burned-out and used-up pastor." By the end of the second day of training, he was in tears. During a coaching session, he had a breakthrough:

Dave: I have been blaming my former congregation for being blind and unwilling to change, but I am the one who is beginning to see.

Coach: What are you seeing?

Dave: How I locked out the congregation from the vision experience. I was so busy telling them what the vision was that I failed to listen to them. It's dawning on me that had I stopped and listened to their hopes and dreams for the church that I might have saved everyone a lot of hurt.

Coach: What do you want to do with this new insight?

Dave: I came here looking for a way out of the pastorate, but now I'm thinking that I need to become a new kind of pastor.

Coach: What kind of pastor would that be?

Dave: One who values the congregation enough to actually listen instead of just stepping in and assuming they need me to come up with all of the answers.

Coach: I notice your language has shifted from you "*having been* a pastor" to you "being a *new kind* of pastor."

Dave: Yes. That's right.

Coach: What will that mean for you?

Dave: It means that God is not finished with me as a pastor. In fact, a church from the other side of the state recently inquired about me sending them my resume. I had planned to ignore the request, but instead I am going to prayerfully send the resume and see what happens.

Coach: What would you like to happen?

Dave: Whether it's with this particular church or another one, I am going to listen to who they are, what God is telling them, and be open to their ideas for what God has in store. When I think about it, what a relief that I don't have to have all the answers. ▪

Managing: A Coach Approach to Organizational Leadership

Many leadership gurus make a clear distinction between leading and managing. One common distinction asserts, "Leaders do the right things, while managers do things right." That is, leaders set the direction for an organization, while managers help the organization move in that direction with efficiency and effectiveness.

An unmistakable message often bubbles through whenever this distinction is made: leadership is "good," and management is "necessary." Leadership is painted in romantic strokes, while management is presented as something that must be done—preferably by someone other than the leader. Management is grunt work, while leadership is where the real fun is. Nothing could be further from the truth, and coaching can help return some respect to management.

The truth is that leaders must develop effective management skills. While the distinction between management and leadership is noteworthy, most leaders fulfill the management function. This is even more true for leaders of churches, small businesses, and not-for-profit organizations. Management helps people follow. While leadership can discern and cast vision all day long, management inspires and equips people to fulfill the vision as part of an organization. Several of Christ's parables involve managers who are shrewd. He recognizes that good management is a positive attribute. Leaders often have to manage. Coaching can help leaders manage well.

A Few Things Leaders Need to Know

Marcus Buckingham boiled leadership and management down to a few key principles. He said that a great leader engages a group of diverse people and communicates that which is universal to the group in clear and compelling ways. In almost direct contrast, a great manager finds what is unique in each person and brings it to bear on the particular outcome needed from that person. Using Buckingham's concepts of leading and managing, consider how coaching can buoy each of these practices.

A manager brings out the best from each person managed to affect the organization positively. A manager is a keen observer of the distinctive resources (strengths, skills, habits, personality, knowledge, preferences, etc.) a person possesses and helps this unique person become a better contributor. As Buckingham wrote, poor managers play checkers (every person/piece having the same capacity and same contribution) while great managers play chess (every person/piece having a unique ability and contribution to winning the game).[4]

A manager who wishes to discover the unique resources of those in the organization can use coaching skills. The coaching attitude can help a manager suspend judgment of how a person ought to be wired or what a person ought to contribute. Through listening, asking questions, and engaging in a coach-like relationship, the manager can discover a person's wiring and contribution potential.

The manager as coach typically does not practice pure coaching, especially as it relates to the agenda of a coaching conversation. Often, a manager needs to help a person achieve certain nonnegotiable outcomes, such as selling more cars, finishing a project, teaching a class, or leading a mission trip. The coaching manager distinguishes the needed outcome from the methods for achieving the outcome. By separating outcomes from methods, the manager can coach around methods while being more directive as to outcomes.

■ ■ ■ Steve, an editor for a major periodical, constantly underperformed. He turned in projects late and poorly done, causing his manager to question Steve's fit for the position. Steve's managing editor began to coach him around his methods for working. Projects still had to be submitted by certain deadlines, and Steve's responsibilities could not be altered, as they were central to the position.

---

[4]Marcus Buckingham, *The One Thing You Need to Know About Great Managing, Great Leadership, and Sustained Individual Success* (New York: Free Press, 2005), 81–84.

Through the coaching process, they co-discovered that Steve's extroverted personality made it difficult for him to concentrate in his small isolated office located in the magazine's central office building. Through a series of coaching conversations, Steve determined which tasks had to be done in the office (e-mail, team meetings, phone calls, and some paperwork) and which tasks could be done at the coffee shop across the street or other public areas where the energy of people contributed to his effectiveness.

They soon discovered that Steve's capacity for editing tripled when he was out of the office. He was able to complete necessary tasks; his work was of higher quality; he was also able to do more work as a result of getting out of the office. Plus, the other editors on staff needed the isolation the office provided and became more productive since chatty Steve was now working offsite much of the time. ■

Moving beyond the workplace, coaching is an especially effective approach for managing individuals and ministry teams. In the church context, ministry leaders can use coaching to bring out the best in those who help carry out ministry. The coach approach to management enables the ministry leader to contribute to the success of volunteers and staff who are charged with accomplishing certain outcomes while helping those being managed feel a strong sense of responsibility, commitment, ownership, and empowerment.

Rather than management by "telling," the coaching manager utilizes asking and listening to help the person or team discover the best path to the desired outcome.

■ ■ ■ A new church plant had a hospitality team that served coffee and greeted first-time guests. This new church put a premium on welcoming newcomers, and the hospitality team played the central role in this. The team wanted to improve the ministry and went to the pastor for advice and help. The pastor had some ideas but decided to take a coach approach. Through several questions about what was working and what needed work, the pastor listened as the team soon discovered some ideas for improving the ministry. The pastor led the team to get specific about what actions needed to be taken and by when to move the ministry forward. After one meeting, a team member commented to the pastor, "We came to you for answers, and all you gave us were questions. But I sure like the results of your questions!" ■

Shepherding: A Coach Approach to Relational Leadership

The traditional image of shepherding is integral to understanding pastoral ministry, even as the world moves deeper into the third millennium.

Though current leadership conversations might imply that pastors are charged with overseeing an organization, the truth is that Christian ministry leaders are ultimately charged with caring for the flock. Ministry leaders care for people.

Though the metaphor breaks down after a while—people are not sheep, and a pastor is not of a different species altogether from the flock—the metaphor proves helpful for understanding a pastor's role. The shepherd moves the flock to where they have food, water, and safety. The move is often challenging, but it may also be necessary for provision. The shepherd cares for the flock and does whatever is necessary for its protection and prosperity.

Pastors care for the flock in terms of leading people through life's passages. Pastors help people deal well with struggles and successes so that they remain on the journey with God, finding protection and provision in relationship with God through Christ. Pastors help people make good decisions, head in the right direction, avoid that which will hurt them, and take advantage of that which will provide sustenance.

Unfortunately, many people think of church and their pastor only when dealing with problems. Church truly is for those in need, but need is not always a negative experience. Pastors who care for their flock via coaching will increase their capacity for care and will be approached by parishioners who face positive life experiences. Pastors can support parishioners with hopes, not just hurts; coaching can open up these new shepherding possibilities.

Coaching's Impact on Shepherding

How does coaching impact the shepherding of a congregation? Coaching and shepherding are not synonymous. Yet there can be a coach approach to shepherding. Coaching can round out the practice of pastoral care, which often focuses on counseling, consulting, and/or chaplaincy.

Consider the distinctions between counseling, consulting, chaplaincy, and coaching. (For additional information, see appendix 1, "Distinctions of Coaching," p. 125.) Each of these is a powerful and effective aspect of shepherding. One cannot be substituted for the other. In simple terms, the four can be distinguished as follows:

- *Counseling* is about therapy and healing from the past. All individuals lug around "baggage." This unnecessary and unhealthy weight creates relational, spiritual, and emotional drag and keeps people from being fully alive. Counseling explores the past to shine light on the past and heal wounds so a person can live more effectively in the now.
- *Chaplaincy* deals with life's passages. This is a ministry of presence and care rooted in the here and now. Though chaplaincy often helps people face death or deal with being in the midst of danger or hurt, chaplaincy spans far beyond that. The pastor as chaplain meets people where they are and helps them think theologically about their situation

to experience the moment more fully. Such life experiences include sickness, danger, and even death. Also included are experiences such as birth, marriage, baptism, graduation, retirement, job promotions, empty nest, divorce, and other life passages.

- *Consulting* is about giving advice. Pastors can serve as experts who offer advice to parishioners and others who are seeking insight into how to approach life. Such expertise has two sources: Scripture and life experience. Pastors who know the Scriptures well may help people search the Bible for guidance. Pastors also can draw on a wealth of their own experiences, the experiences of other parishioners, and what the church has taught on a particular matter to help someone think through an issue with greater insight. Consulting (of which mentoring is a form) is an appropriate means of helping people who face similar life-issues and who can find value in knowing what has worked for others. Great consulting also knows its own limitations: expertise and advice cannot be imposed, should be restricted to only those situations in which the experiences are similar, and should often be paired alongside another helping approach, such as coaching, chaplaincy, or counseling.

- *Coaching* is about caring for a person's future. Counseling looks to the past to find healing. Chaplaincy looks toward heaven to find truth for here and now. Consulting looks to the pastor as an expert to solve problems and answer questions. Coaching is distinctive in that it looks upward (to God), inward (to one's self as impacted by the indwelling of God's Spirit), and forward (to where God is leading) to find direction for tomorrow. Coaching, like pastoral care, is about helping people make good decisions and take action that truly moves them forward.

The pastor who uses coaching will want to be discerning as to when to apply a coach approach to shepherding. To misapply will do harm. The parishioner who needs therapy will be unable to look inwardly with effectiveness and will design poor plans for the future because of the inner dysfunction that requires healing. The parishioner who is dealing with death or another life passage does not necessarily need an action plan. Likewise, to miss a coaching opportunity and misapply counseling, chaplaincy, or consulting when coaching is needed will provide less-than-best results.

Conditions for Coaching as Pastoral Care

When is coaching the right way to provide shepherding? Consider the following guidelines for recognizing coaching possibilities:

- The parishioner displays no obvious need for therapy or healing.
- The parishioner uses language focused more on today and the future, revealing that energy and attention are focused more forward than back.

- The parishioner is faced with a tough decision.
- The parishioner is stuck in a holding pattern that requires a new approach, a new strategy, or even a new paradigm. Sometimes developing new paradigms can begin to include some counseling skills if the current paradigm is based on past hurts. This is not always the case. Many paradigms are simply the ways that people have chosen to look at life and do not require healing to be altered.
- The parishioner has a vision for a better future but is unsure how to get there.
- The parishioner has a challenge that requires intentional action.
- The parishioner faces an opportunity that requires personal action.

■ ■ ■ With a disheveled appearance and demeanor, Kerri rushed through the doors of the church for an evening meeting. Her pastor, Carlos, asked her if everything was okay. Kerri brushed off the question by responding, "No, but it's nothing you can help me with. It's just that work and family and other commitments are about to swallow me whole. You know how life can be!"

Carlos agreed that life could sometimes seem overwhelming and encouraged Kerri to rethink whether her condition was outside a minister's charge. He briefly described coaching to her and then invited her to invest thirty minutes the next day for a coaching session via phone. She agreed and called the next afternoon.

Using Gary Collins's coaching model (see p. 62), Carlos led Kerri to explore her life imbalance using the model as a framework. Through a series of questions and responses, Kerri realized two things: Christ was only a slice of her life, not the center, and she did not have a strategy for managing competing forces in her life. Since they had agreed to only a thirty-minute conversation and lacked the time needed to make a major life overhaul, Carlos encouraged Kerri to find a "baby step" forward based on her two realizations.

Kerri quickly determined to refocus herself on the person of Christ by committing to reading a chapter from the gospel of John each day for the next two weeks and to reflect on how each passage could place Christ more at the center of her life. She also committed to keeping a two-week log of when her various commitments collided in order that she might be able to recognize patterns and make adjustments. At the end of the conversation, Kerri asked Carlos for another coaching session, and they scheduled a phone appointment for two weeks later. ■

Conclusion

Coaching is a powerful way of relating that can increase a ministry leader's effectiveness. Great leaders will use coaching as one tool in the leadership toolbox. Yet, the tool is not an unusual one. Coaching is more like a screwdriver or monkey wrench—tools that are needed often and used frequently—than a pair of wire cutters or an adz—tools that are needed only in special circumstances and used rarely.

For ministry leaders, coaching can provide a warm and theologically grounded approach to leading. Pastors and other ministry leaders who engage in visioning, managing, and shepherding should find coaching useful. Though coaching is not synonymous with leadership, visioning, managing, or shepherding, it supports each of these practices and should enable ministry leaders to practice leadership with greater effectiveness.

A Prayer for Leaders Who Use Coaching

God, You are our Leader. Your influence is felt with each breath we take, each sunrise we experience, each emotion we feel, each relationship we are in, and each Scripture we read.

For those whom You've called to lead congregations, offer Your grace and truth in extra abundance. The vocation of ministry is special in so many ways. Your help is needed. May the practice of coaching be one of the blessings You offer to those who lead in Your name as well as a means by which You bless those who are led. May church leaders serve as relational conduits by which people are led by You, toward You, for Your glory and our good. And may coaching expand our capacity for bringing You to bear in the lives of those we lead. We ask this in Your Son's name, Amen.

Beyond the Book

1. From your knowledge and review of Scripture, what are some biblical instances of God or Jesus taking a "coach approach" to leading His people? What specific learnings can you apply from these examples?
2. Beyond those mentioned in this chapter, what other ministry leadership roles do you see that coaching can impact?
3. Consider what real life experiences would be examples of the need for counseling, chaplaincy, and coaching.
4. How do the lessons in this chapter (which lean heavily toward ministry leaders) apply to Christian leaders who exercise influence in business, community, family, or other non-ecclesial contexts?
5. Think of one leader who could benefit from taking more of a coach approach. How would coaching improve that person's leadership?
6. What aspect of your leadership needs special attention? What are three ways your leadership can improve through being more coachlike?

7

Coaching in the Church

■ ■ ■ Claire is a mother of three who works part-time in the engineering department of a major telecommunications company. On a Sunday evening in early May, she and her husband, Tony, looked out over the coming week's set of obligations. They had a play date for their preschooler, a church committee meeting one evening, a retirement party for one of Claire's managers, gifts to buy and trips to be made for Mother's Day, and two end-of-the-year school parties for their school-age children. The coming week looked familiarly busy, stretching them from one set of obligations to another. They longed for fewer obligations and more meaningful relationships. ■

In a recent book on relationships, Randy Frazee led his readers to draw circles representing their communities and connect them to one another with lines to represent natural social flow. The aim of the exercise was to demonstrate that Westerners in the beginning of the third millennium have way too many communities to navigate effectively. Rather than give buoyancy to life, these overlapping, contradicting, and splintered "communities" sink people in overcommitments and fractured relationships.[1]

Coaching and Community

Today people live with more relationships but less true community than perhaps ever before. This has three things to do with Christian coaching. First, while action is a key emphasis in coaching and is near the

---

[1]Randy Frazee, *Making Room for Life: Trading Chaotic Lifestyles for Connected Relationships* (Grand Rapids: Zondervan, 2004).

heart of effectiveness, coaching underscores that humans are designed for relationships. Our essence is relational. Like our Trinitarian Creator, we are made for being with one another. Coaching is a relationship.

Second, if relationships are so important, which relational community provides the best opportunity for whole, healthy, and God-oriented relationships? The answer is church. People who are connected to God through Christ are also most connected to one another. Many churches fall woefully short when it comes to relationships, but this does not change the truth of what Bill Hybels has so often stated: "The local church is the hope of the world."[2] Church—that universally ordered and locally expressed community of Christ-followers—is the only community for true relationship because it is the one community impacted by and centered on Christ's atoning work. So, for all of its shortcomings, church is our main context for relating.

Third, coaching fits into this conversation because coaching gives boost to church relationships. If church is more than a building and a set of programs—if church is the community of Christ-followers who are doing life together—then coaching energizes the relating that is central to church.

This chapter will explore how coaching can impact the three relational aims of church: Christians' relationship to God in worship, Christians' relationships to each other in community, and Christians' relationship to the world in mission.

Coaching and Worship

People connect to God through worship. Through worship, God makes Himself available to His followers; and it is the believer's privilege to enter into ongoing relationship with God by giving God honor, glory, praise, and sacrifice. Church leaders facilitate worship through at least four practices: preaching, the sacraments of baptism and communion, and prayer. Coaching can have a significant positive impact on each.

A Coach Approach to Preaching and Proclaiming

■ ■ ■ Pastor Greg had invested Friday and Saturday in a seminary workshop on coaching. On his drive home Saturday evening, his excitement about this new and powerful way of relating had his mind racing. He wondered how he might work coaching into his Sunday morning sermon. "That's crazy," he thought, "it's too late to rework tomorrow's sermon. After all, people will just think that I've been to some minister's meeting and am trying to tell them everything I learned by hijacking the sermon."

As he drove, he went over the sermon and Scripture in his mind. The New Testament reading came from John 5 about the

---

[2]Bill Hybels, *Courageous Leadership* (Grand Rapids: Zondervan, 2002), 21.

man Jesus healed by the pool of Bethesda. Then it struck him: "Do you want to get well?" Jesus asked the man a powerful question! His mind quickly connected several dots:

• this Scripture passage told of an encounter with some real coaching moments;
• his own sermons could have coaching moments;
• the key was to incorporate powerful questions that lead to actions that help people "get well" by committing more and more to Christ and Christlikeness;
• the sermon should not be about coaching, but should use coaching.

The next morning, he drew the sermon to a close by asking three powerful and precise questions that moved people to consider action. The following week, he received four e-mails from parishioners who had taken specific actions as a result of the sermon. Greg had found new life for his preaching. ■

A coach approach can impact preaching in at least four ways.

First, coaching can remind the preacher to seek a balance between asking and telling. A minister committed to coaching can quickly get uncomfortable with preaching because preaching seems to be all about telling people what to believe and do. Yet preachers can effectively ask powerful preaching questions.

Jesus was a Master at using powerful questions to elicit discovery, commitment, and understanding among those in His presence. Though scholars debate whether Jesus frequently "preached" in the manner that ministers do today, He obviously used words for teaching, proclaiming, and engaging. As Conrad Gempf explored, most of Jesus' interaction, both in words and deeds, had a questioning effect.[3] Jesus used questions, parables, and other oratory approaches to help people discover and decide for themselves who Jesus was. Through His ministry Jesus showed people who He was; through His words He asked them who He was. This is powerfully seen in the brief exchange with the disciples, when Jesus pointedly asked, "Who do you say I am?"(Mt. 16:15), and Peter answered. Gempf concluded that nearly all of Jesus' ministry revolved around "asking" people to identify their understanding of who He was. Modeling Jesus' ministry, contemporary preachers can balance sermons with less telling and more asking.

Think about It: _____

✦ How many of Jesus' questions can you recall from memory?

✦ Do a quick survey through the New Testament and take note of the questions of Jesus.

---

[3]Conrad Gempf, *Jesus Asked: What He Wanted to Know* (Grand Rapids: Zondervan, 2003).

It may be helpful to explore what powerful preaching questions *do not* look like. Here are some guidelines for what to avoid.

- *Rhetorical questions.* Because many preaching venues are not conducive to people blurting out audible responses, some preachers assume preaching questions should be rhetorical—that is, a question that does not anticipate an answer. But powerful preaching questions should elicit a response. Though the response may not be verbalized, preaching questions do not have to be rhetorical. Rhetorical questions are typically not powerful. To avoid empty rhetoric and encourage actual response, preachers can ask congregants to write their responses or to share responses with someone sitting nearby or with someone later that day.

- *Leading questions.* Preachers should not ask people questions that lead people to say what the preachers want to hear. Leading questions feel like a trap, and questions should free people to discover truth, not trap them in a corner where they are not free to choose.

- *Closed-ended questions.* The answer(s) to these questions cannot be obvious. There cannot be a right or wrong answer. Again, congregants need freedom to choose a response or discover an answer. Closed-ended questions usually do not result in discovery of something new but, rather, force a choice among known options (Yes or No? This or That? A, B, C, or D?). Occasionally, closed-ended questions can be powerful, but they tend to be manipulative and narrowing, especially when used in preaching.

- *Rapid-fire questions.* Asking question after question without time for thought or for response underscores that the questions are rhetorical and not intended for serious consideration. When people are bombarded with too many questions, the truly great questions can get ignored because of the overwhelming amount of questions.

Powerful preaching questions result in discovery, new understanding, fresh commitments, and a desire to behave differently. They can work well in preaching.

Tips for Making Questions Work Well in Preaching

✻ Give time for response. Good coaching is comfortable with silence and reflection.

✻ Give opportunity for response. The coaching skill of "identifying action" helps congregants know how to respond. Sometimes, the response is internal, and the appropriate response is for listeners to think through their response. Other times, congregants can be encouraged to turn and share their responses with someone nearby, to share with someone in the coming day or week, or to write the response in a visible place at home or office.

✳ Using questions powerfully does not always mean asking only powerful questions. For example, the question, "What place would you like to visit?" is a low-risk and, admittedly, low-reward question. But such questions can create a context for dialogue and can introduce congregants to thinking, responding, and interacting so that they are ready for a more powerful question later.

✳ Emphasize action. All good preaching has a "So what?" factor. Rather than tell people what to do, questions provoke action tailored to each person. Questions can help congregants discover what to do based on the lesson.

Here are sample questions gleaned from actual sermons:

• "This woman who was brought before Jesus had been caught in the shameful and potentially disastrous act of adultery. If you knew Jesus would offer forgiveness and healing, what shameful act would you allow Jesus 'to catch' you doing?"

• "The blind man was given sight, but it was only partial at first. He told Jesus that he saw men, but that they looked like trees. When it comes to the new life you are finding in Christ, what seems only partially complete?"

• "If you could vacation or visit any place in the world, where would it be? (*pause*) What is it about that place that draws you? (*longer pause*) How could this place be a metaphor for where Christ wants to take you in your spiritual journey?"

• "Jesus said that He came to give us 'abundant life.' What would that look like for you right now?"

• "Thomas doubted that Christ had really been resurrected. Based on your experience with Christ and His church, what are your biggest doubts?"

• "When pushed by Jesus, Peter confessed that Jesus was, 'The Messiah, the Son of the Living God.' Based on your encounter with Jesus and in your own words, who do you say Jesus is?"

A Coach Approach to Sacraments

Many Christian traditions have a set of highly important practices called "sacraments" or "ordinances." Coaching can positively impact the already meaningful practices of baptism and communion. The following suggestions should spark your creativity so you can adjust and adapt for your tradition.

For nearly two thousand years, Christians have practiced baptism. It is one of the few practices that unites Christians who are otherwise incredibly diverse. Coaching can impact the practice of baptism on a number of levels.

First, for those traditions that practice believer's baptism, the minister can coach the baptismal candidate to have a deeper understanding and appreciation of the act. Alongside the appropriate teaching about baptism, the minister can help the candidate assign personal meaning to the experience. In essence, a coach approach helps the person being baptized understand the experience at a deeper level and discover new and fresh ways of appropriating the act into everyday Christian living.

In addition to pre-baptism coaching, the minister can offer or suggest post-baptism coaching to help the new believer live out the faith. For traditions that practice believer's baptism, the new life born through faith in Christ entails a radical shift in one's approach to life. Coaching is perfectly suited for helping people deal effectively with life transitions, and being "born again" (Jn. 3) is a significant life transition. Coaching can help new converts take tangible steps in following Christ as a direct after-effect of baptism. These coaching engagements could simply be one-session coaching experiences, though a more powerful coaching engagement might include six to eight sessions that help new converts gain traction in living out the new lives they have in Christ.

Deepen the Learning and Forward the Action

The Coaches Training Institute bases most of its coach training on the Co-Active Coaching Model developed by Laura Whitworth and Henry Kimsey-House. Their concept of coaching includes the helpful notion that each coaching conversation both "deepens the learning and forwards the action." A coach approach to worship will carry this same twofold aim. Deepened understanding and appreciation of God, sacraments, and prayer should lead to action that forwards the kingdom in the life of the believers. As the biblical book James (1:22-23) says, it is important that we be not just hearers of the word, but also doers. Coaching can help with hearing (especially as it relates to understanding) as well as with doing.[4]

For traditions that baptize children or infants, coaching can create a better supporting community for the child. Parents, godparents, and congregants who commit to rearing the child in Christ and toward Christ can be coached to carry out this important role more effectively. For example, during many baptismal services, attendees verbally commit to nurturing the child in the faith. The minister might prompt each person to wrestle with this role, asking, "How will you help this child remember this baptism?"

Another significant practice of worshiping Christians is communion. This beautiful and ancient practice can also be positively impacted through coaching. Paul advised believers to not partake of the Lord's Supper with a light spirit or unexamined heart (1 Cor. 11). Rather than allowing the

---

[4]Laura Whitworh, Henry Kimsey-House, and Phil Sandahl, *Co-Active Coaching: New Skills for Coaching People Toward Success in Work and Life* (Palo Alto, Calif.: Davies-Black, 1998), 5–6.

reflection, confession, and repentance that precede bread and wine to be empty ritual, coaching can give additional traction to the ritual so that each participant more fully prepares for the experience of communing with Christ.

Ministers can encourage deep reflection through using powerful questions and appropriate listening. For example, giving congregants one question on which to reflect during prayer can help guide their time in preparing for the sacrament. Ministers can also use the coaching tool of metaphor to guide reflection and as a vehicle for powerful questions. Here are some examples of coaching questions to use around communion:

- As we prepare to take Christ's body and blood into our very selves, reflect on what else you have taken in recently–through your eyes, your ears, your will, or your mind–that you'd like Christ to replace.
- Having taken in Christ and expelled sin, what is one way you will commit to living in Christ and not sin this week?
- As a way of entering into communion with a clean heart, commit right now to having that one conversation that you know you need to have for Christ to be powerfully alive in you. Who is that person? When will you have that conversation? Quietly say the first words of that conversation right now.
- Partaking of Christ's body and blood is a very powerful way of expressing our faith in Him and His provision for us. Knowing that Christ will provide, that He will come through, and that you can trust Him, what is one more way you can express your faith in Him this coming week?

A Coach Approach to Prayer

Prayer takes on many forms in Christians' lives. From ancient prayers recited en masse to spontaneous utterances offered by an individual, prayer is communication with God. With such a variety of prayer possibilities, can coaching meaningfully impact the practice?

While coaching may not revolutionize prayer, coaching can aid in the understanding of prayer. In short, prayer is like coaching in a few notable ways.

First, coaching develops an appreciation for intentional conversations. Conversation is inherent in prayer. Coaches are quick to listen, and coaching makes people better conversationalists, whether conversing with one another or with the Almighty. Teaching people to pray may look a lot like teaching people to coach.

Second, coaching focuses on helping people reach new levels of understanding, insights, and perspectives. The same is true for prayer. A coach approach to prayer emphasizes that prayer time may change beliefs, attitudes, and understandings. Something new will develop in the person praying as a result of time spent in prayer. Prayer is not an instant-reward kind of conversation. Prayer is a deeply mysterious and marvelous Christian practice, yet it is a practice that changes hearts and minds.

Third, coaching emphasizes action. Prayer is not action, but it is often the prelude to action. A believer's time with God often moves that person to act differently: to repent, confess, cease, start, better live a life oriented to Christ. As a reorienting enterprise, prayer should lead to adjustments in the believer's life, which are expressed in new, better, and different actions.

Fourth, coaching places power in the relationship, not in one or other of the parties involved. While this may sound like the antithesis of a prayer that submits to God, it is not. As Eugene Peterson suggests, those who pray should avoid the extremes of being totally active or totally passive. One who prays with total activity commands God and makes God a holy butler who follows our orders. The one who prays with total passivity makes God a holy commander who barks orders to be followed. Peterson advised believers to be both active and passive with God. In prayer, "We neither manipulate God (active voice) nor are manipulated by God (passive voice). We are involved in the action and participate in its results but do not control or define it (middle voice). Prayer takes place in the middle voice."[5]

Coaching gives an excellent earthly example of what this kind of prayer is like. Coaches bring power to the relationship, as do those who are being coached. Like a great coach, God's number one agenda is to help the praying person identify and accomplish a personal agenda that is tied to God's greater purposes. Like a good coaching session, time in prayer involves the praying person actively submitting to a conversation of trust and hope with God.

Coaching and Building Community with One Another

■ ■ ■ Rick and Carl met with three other men every Tuesday morning for breakfast and Bible study. Carl had recently gone through some coach training through his employer and planned to start coaching the people who reported directly to him. But on this particular Tuesday morning, he saw the value of coaching even friends like Rick.

As the group explored the tenth chapter of Mark, Rick wondered out loud about Jesus' pronouncement concerning divorce that "a man will leave his father and mother and be united to his wife." A coaching exchange resulted.

Rick: "This passage makes me think about my relationship with Kerri." (*his wife*)

---

[5]Eugene Peterson, *The Contemplative Pastor: Returning to the Art of Spiritual Direction* (Grand Rapids: Eerdmans, 1993), 104.

Carl: "How so?" (*Recalling his coach training, Carl did not jump to the assumption that Rick and Kerri were considering divorce.*)

Rick: "She and I have been talking lately about our relationship and how it could be better."

Carl: "What have you come up with?" (*Carl did not take Rick to "what was wrong," but followed Rick to talk about what could be better.*)

Rick: "Well, Kerri thinks that I have not fully left my mother and father, kind of like this passage talks about."

Carl: "What do you think?"

Rick: "My first instinct is that Kerri is totally off-base. I mean, I'm no mama's boy or anything like that. We've been married for eight years, and we are obviously 'united.'"

Carl: "So that's your first instinct. What are your more developed thoughts?"

Rick: "Yeah, I think my knee-jerk reaction is that she's wrong, but I can also see where she's coming from. I guess a few habits of mine could make Kerri think that I pay more attention to my parents than I do to her. I probably need to work on it." (*At this point, Rick's demeanor demonstrated that he was ready for the focus to shift to someone else. In keeping with the normal operating procedure of the group, he had shared a nebulous issue and given a general "I need to work on that" solution. But Carl decided to press for just a bit more.*)

Carl: "You know Rick, it takes a lot of courage to even be open to the idea that your wife might be right and that you need to work on some habits. If you were to change one habit, which one would you start with?"

Rick: (*pleasantly surprised by the question*) "Hmmm. Truth is, I don't have to think about that at all. The one big habit is about making plans. When mom and dad want to see the kids or have us visit, I am all the time making plans without first consulting Kerri. She doesn't mind the visits, but she really gets irked at not being in the decision-making loop. She says that it makes her feel like she's just one of the kids."

Carl: "So what can you do differently?"

Rick: "From now on, when it comes to planning visits, I am going to say to my parents, 'Let me check with Kerri.'"

Carl: "That sounds like a workable plan. What would make that even better?"

Rick: "Do you have something in mind?"

Carl: "Nope. I just figure you are a guy who loves his wife and children, respects his parents, and wants to have solid relationship between everybody and that there's likely something that will take a very good plan to the next level and make it great."

Rick: "You're right. The thing that would make this even better is to have Kerri talk with my parents. They have a good relationship, and I think that they can figure out when visits can happen. The truth is, I don't really care about that kind of thing; and so having them talk would keep me from being the middle man and would help them form an even stronger relationship. In fact, on my way into work, I am going to call Kerri and get her input into this. I think she'll be excited and will appreciate this 'new habit.'"

From that morning forward, the Tuesday morning Bible study took on a coaching tone, with at least one man being coached at each gathering. Eventually, the other men learned from Carl how to ask precise questions, how to listen, and how to utilize the other coaching skills. Each of them not only moved forward, but also were each granted a front-row seat into one another's life. Their community strengthened as a result. ▪

In addition to connecting with God, believers are empowered and called to connect with one another. Through the power of Christ, believers are enabled to know and be known. Believers are called to live in communion with God and in community with one another.

Though coaching is sometimes portrayed as an individual pursuit of individual aims, Christian coaching can support the formation of community. The power of coaching to bring forth truth, negotiate meaningful action, and deepen understanding makes it an ally of community. Coaching can support community formation and excellence by getting beyond the surface, promoting spiritual growth, and encouraging spiritual friendship. These themes are not programs that can be propped up by coaching, but relationships that can benefit from coaching.

Moving beyond the Surface–Getting to What Matters Most through Coaching

Much of what passes for Christian community these days goes barely beyond niceties, civilized and safe conversation and pretense. Sunday school and small groups wrestle to get beneath surface discussions and beyond fill-in-the-blank conversations. Fellowship involves "meaningful" conversations about basketball, weather, and the merits of the meal we share. While there is a place for polite conversation, how can relationships evolve into something significant? Coaching can assist parishioners in developing the Christian practices of hospitality and conflict.

Hospitality

Christian community begins with hospitality–opening home, hearth, and heart to others. While today's Western culture has perfected the anti-Christian practice of "cocooning," some Christians are rediscovering the ancient practice of hospitality. Coaching can ignite and support hospitality among Christians by developing coaching attitudes and abilities.

Coaching develops an attitude of serving others without being used. Wise coaches go to great lengths for the person being coached but know the boundary between helpful service and enabling "suffering." Coaching promotes an attitude that is other-centered while avoiding inappropriate martyrdom. Coaches offer themselves as servants to others, providing meaningful dialogue without being spent of all energy and resource. As one coaching book title put it, coaching is about heart and backbone.[6]

Christians who practice hospitality can also take the coaching attitude of being a servant who is not taken advantage of. George C. Hunter III described the hospitality of the ancient Celts.[7] They welcomed strangers and the needy into their midst, giving refuge and resources. Yet, they did not allow strangers to take over or demand.

Four Levels of Intimacy

To invite others into your life does not look the same for everyone. In fact, finding the right level of intimacy is important. Edward T. Hall describes four types of social space: public, social, personal, intimate. Each type carries its own reward and is tailored for different relationships. Coaching offers a powerful means for discerning in what space a relationship exists, what forms of hospitality are appropriate for a given relationship, and what might be helpful for moving the relationship forward. By utilizing great coaching questions and focused listening, the believer can be intentional and on target with hospitality in service to the Christian community.[8]

Christians who practice hospitality can open home, hearth, and heart to others in a way that ensures home, hearth, and heart remain intact. Hospitality is not the same as welcoming an invasion!

A coach attitude toward hospitality involves three coaching confessions:

- *I am not the servant; the relationship I provide is the servant.* Since the power of coaching is in the relationship (not in the coach), believers should seek to engage others in relationship. This truth calls Christians out of cocoons and into purposeful time invested with others. It does not call believers to endlessly extend, which actually is not very helpful. As strange as it might sound, this coaching principle teaches

---

[6]Mary Beth O'Neill, *Executive Coaching with Backbone and Heart: A Systems Approach to Engaging Leaders with Their Challenges* (San Francisco: Jossey-Bass, 2000).

[7]George C. Hunter III, *The Celtic Way of Evangelism: How Christianity Can Reach the West...Again* (Nashville: Abingdon Press, 2000).

[8]Joseph Myers, *The Search to Belong: Rethinking Intimacy, Community, and Small Groups* (Grand Rapids: Zondervan, 2003).

that when others are invited into a home for a meal, the guests help clean up the dirty dishes! Life together as expressed in hospitality involves co-equals sharing life, doing life together, and being partners.

- *I am not called to fix the other person, but to provide relationship.* Coaches are listeners, questioners, conversationalists, thought partners, and even challengers. Coaches avoid becoming fixers. Hospitality is more about providing an environment than a cure. The end of hospitality is not a cure toward which the relationship is the means. The healthy relationship is the end. Coaching skills of listening and being actively present provide modern-day support, refuge, relief, and safety for those in our midst.

- *I do harm when I allow others to abuse or mistreat me.* Coaches can easily succumb to the temptation of letting others dump their problems on the coach. However, wise coaches learn to help others own what is theirs and provide support as others sort through problems and opportunities. This principle can be applied to the practice of hospitality. Allowing others to be leeches is not helpful to them. When people invade or otherwise act inappropriately, the giver of hospitality must call such behavior for what it is. The coaching skills of establishing the relationship and truth telling support this aspect of hospitality.

Conflict

Things don't always go smoothly when it comes to doing life together. Even emotionally intelligent people have conflict. Coaching can help Christians deal with conflict well by giving us new skills and attitudes.

First, coaching gives the skills to speak well with one another. Coaching can help people avoid unnecessary personal conflict by being intentional with words and working toward greater clarity. The wonderful coaching expression, "Explain what you mean by that," or, "Say more about that," serves any relationship, not just those marked as coaching. Offered with humility and a nonjudgmental spirit, inquiries that seek to gain greater clarity help people avoid jumping to inaccurate conclusions and into resulting conflict.

Second, coaching helps people work through differences with its attitude of healthy detachment. In one sense, this happens when coaches detach themselves from outcomes and opinions. So many conflicts in Christian life come over simple disagreements when believers could healthily agree to disagree. The ability to live in disagreement requires a level of maturity that is wonderfully imaged in coaching. Coaches are men and women who've had an "Aha!" that changes their approach to life. Coaches can let people live their lives instead of imposing a specific life on them. The healthy detachment that is learned and practiced in coaching can help people move through many conflicts.

Spiritual Growth

For the past twenty or so years, Christian leaders have expressed a renewed emphasis on spiritual growth. For the most part, this is a welcomed focus of attention. However, much of what has been regarded as "spiritual growth" is a relationally disconnected pursuit. A coach approach to spiritual growth can have rich rewards as it provides a relational basis for the pursuit of Christlikeness.

To fuel this conversation about the relationship of coaching and spiritual growth, consider three useful definitions of faith provided by Marcus Borg.[9] These definitions are based on three Latin terms that often get translated as "faith" by English speakers. The following table outlines the three concepts.

Three Concepts of Faith

Type	Description	Examples	Opposites
Assensus	Accept as true	• Accepting historicity of Christ's resurrection • Wrestling to fathom "God loves you" • Accepting the Bible to be authoritative	• Mild—doubt or skepticism • Harsher— disbelief
Fidelitas	Faithfulness or fidelity	• Relational commitment to God • Similar to trust given to a spouse in marriage • Faithfulness to the relationship itself	• Unfaithfulness • Adultery • Idolatry
Fiducia	Trust	• Radical trust in God • Give concerns of life over to God • "I don't know how this is going to work out, but I know God is in control."	• Mistrust • Anxiety

Much of what passes for spiritual growth is faith largely from the *assensus* angle. While facts and truth claims are important aspects of faithfulness, this approach often leads to lots of "head knowledge" but not much life change. An emphasis on *assensus* relies less on relationship. Contemporary society seems to prefer disembodied truth, teachers, and learning.

---

[9]Adapted from Marcus Borg, *The Heart of Christianity: Rediscovering a Life of Faith* (New York: HarperCollins, 2003), 25–42, and "What Is Faith?" preached March 16, 2001, at Calvary Episcopal Church in Memphis, available online at http://www.explorefaith.org/ LentenHomily03.16.01.html (accessed May 2006).

Coaching provides a means for reestablishing *fidelitas* and *fiducia* aspects of faithfulness to the Christian walk. A coach approach to spiritual growth guides people beyond learning the facts of faith and moves them into living lives of faithfulness to God that rely on God's total provision. These dimensions of faith are not learned apart from relational discipleship. Coaching provides a strong means of relational disciple-making.

Following are some examples of how coaching can impact the spiritual formation of Christ followers:

- *Spiritual Life Coaches.* Some congregations are training staff and lay volunteers to serve as spiritual life coaches for fellow congregants. These spiritual life coaches enter into coaching relationships with others to aid them in their journeys toward Christlikeness. These one-on-one relationships provide a formal and friendly dialogue with a precise outcome in mind: spiritual growth that is expressed in changed behavior.
- *Small Groups.* Other congregations are training persons involved in small groups to add a coaching element to group conversation. These "coaching catalysts" may or may not be the small group leaders. They move the conversation beyond learning and toward behavior, ensuring each small group participant clearly has a take-away learning that will be expressed in action. These small group coaches are excellent action negotiators. They are also splendid listeners who tie together the curriculum experience, varying life experiences, and the challenge to live like Christ to garner tangible commitments from small group members.
- *Sunday School.* Like those in a small group environment, persons in a more formal Christian education setting can benefit from a coaching presence. Curriculum can be supplemented with powerful questions. Many questions in Sunday school curriculum either provoke thought but not an answer, or provoke an answer but not thought. Class leaders with an appreciation for coaching may want to ask questions that require class members to think deeply to come up with actual answers.
- *Structured Coaching Services.* Many churches offer counseling to those in need of caring and healing relationships. Some churches find that coaching can supplement and even expand their counseling ministries. Parishioners and neighbors whose forward movement does not require healing or therapy can benefit from a structured coaching ministry that provides coaching for life's passages, struggles, and opportunities. Pastors often enjoy providing coaching services to their church members, as it gives them a way of helping build ability within the members. Many pastors schedule coaching sessions with church members who are interested in moving forward in life—be it with "spiritual matters," family, career, or other issues.

Spiritual Friendships

Those involved in coach training sometimes hear the comment, "Coaching sounds a lot like being a good friend." There is much truth to this. Better said, a true friend knows when to demonstrate friendship by acting like a coach and listening intently, asking specific questions, helping the person move forward intentionally, and acknowledging action and next steps. Spiritual friends can use a variety of coaching skills in service to one another.

Many Christ followers and congregations are rediscovering the power and purpose of spiritual friendships: unique relationships that are specifically intended to move one another toward God. In addition to programmatic and scholastic approaches to spiritual growth, spiritual friendships provide an organic and highly relational means for spiritual growth.

Anam Cara—a Soul Friend

The ancient Celts used the term *anam cara* to describe what the Bible calls "a friend who sticks closer than a brother" (Prov. 18:24). Such a spiritual friendship is between two equals who walk alongside each other for the purpose of helping each other grow into the image of Christ. Rather than being a pedagogical approach to discipleship, the soul friendship is a relational approach to growing in faith.

Coaching can bring spiritual intentionality to existing friendships. Churches are full of people who gather for coffee and conversation. They sip coffee (or eat lunch or watch a ballgame) and talk about life. Sometimes these conversations turn to spiritual matters, and sometimes they do not.

Coaching works in these settings because it inherently relies on the power of relationship. Coaching is a relationship of peers, not a relationship in which one party has more power than the other. Coaching is an approach that helps peers bring power to one another without one of the friends "being in charge." Spiritual friends who attempt to be a consultant or mentor are limited to the experience and expertise they have; the relationship runs out of power when these sources are extinguished. But a coach approach to spiritual friendship relies on the power of the relationship, an unlimited and ever-renewing source of energy and experience.

Persons who take a coach approach to life will bring the power of coaching to these relationships by:

1. Realizing that conversations can support movement. Coaches realize that people are constantly moving forward. For Christ followers, this forward movement is oriented by and directed toward God. A spiritual friend with a coach approach will see each conversation as an opportunity to help a friend move toward God. This transforms nice conversations into spiritual growth catalysts.

2. Following the flow of the conversation. Many friends engage in conversation without any real purpose or awareness of how it is flowing. Spiritual friends who take a coach approach will be intentional about helping one another make new discoveries and take new actions.

3. Asking powerful questions. A friendship conversation may not be as full of questions as a formal coaching session, but a good spiritual friend realizes the power of questions and brings that power to bear on the friendship. Replacing three or four comments with powerful questions will transform a conversation.

4. Listening intently. All good friends are great listeners. Too bad we know so few good friends these days! Friends who have a coach approach listen not only to what the other is saying, but also to the relationship itself and to the flow of what is going on in the life of the friend. Rather than getting caught up in the drama or in the moment of what is being experienced (empathy), the friend listens to the other's whole life and places what is being said in the context of that entirety as well as in the context of God's ultimate story.

5. Allowing proper ownership of accountability. Many spiritual friendships stop at accountability partnerships. While mutual accountability can be an important part of a spiritual relationship, coaching moves beyond this dynamic. By placing ultimate accountability and responsibility on the person being coached, coaching encourages each Christ follower to take ownership of the personal journey. This leads to a relationship that is able to get at issues of spiritual growth that are deeper than simply avoiding sin. Such friendships don't focus on, "Did you sin or not?" but move beyond this to, "What's behind your desire to sin?" A coaching-influenced spiritual friendship will be able to address root causes instead of treating surface symptoms.

Coaching and Our Mission to the World

Christians connect with God in worship and connect to each other in Christ-oriented community with one another. Beyond these two connections, Christians, on mission to the world, help others connect to God. Just as with worship and community, there can be a coach approach to mission.

Ministry Teams

Service to the world is work. In Christian vernacular, it is "ministry." It's helpful to think of ministry as work because it underlines the similarities with other endeavors: ministry takes effort and teamwork, and it can be done more or less effectively. This does not understate the active role of the Holy Spirit or the supernatural resources that empower our service to the world, but it acknowledges that Christians' work is not simple or always fun.

Ministry is often best accomplished by teams. "Team" is a bit of a buzzword these days, but the concept goes back to Scripture as people worked together in mission to the world. Teams are action-oriented. Teams are not chiefly about making decisions but are about taking meaningful action. As such, teams thrive with coaching. When ministry teams thrive, so does the ministry offered to the world.

How can coaching help teams? First, coaching can help groups become teams. Many boards, staffs, councils, and committees could function better as teams. Coaching can help these groups re-envision themselves as teams that exist to get things done. Coaching can transform groups into teams in four ways or shifts:

1. *From members to players.* Coaching brings out the best in people, helping them reach their full potential. When coaching is brought to bear on teams, each member becomes an active contributor to the success of the ministry. As emphasis is placed on action and forward progress, each person's identity shifts from "member of the group" to "contributor to the ministry."
2. *From decisions to actions.* Board and committee minutes are full of discussions and decisions. Coaching emphasizes that good decisions lead to action, thus shifting the emphasis to what happens as a result of the meeting, rather than what happened at the meeting.
3. *From internal to external.* Groups often get caught up in the internal workings of the group: how it is organized, who is present, what the rules are, who has certain responsibilities, and so forth. By emphasizing results, coaching shifts focus from the group to what the team accomplishes and whom the team serves.
4. *From procedure to process.* Proper procedure does not always lead to great decisions or effective ministry action. Too often, groups get bogged down in procedures rather than productivity. Coaching provides a process for having productive conversations rather than marking success as "having followed a prescribed procedure."

Second, coaching can help team meetings be more productive. Team meetings are really a group coaching conversation. Central to productive team meetings is how team members relate to one another in meetings. Five healthy attributes mark good teams and are reinforced by coaching:

1. *Trust of one another.* Team members trust one another when they know one another. Knowing one another as real human beings—as husbands or wives, people with hopes and hurts, persons who were once children and who someday may be terminally ill, and as beings created with inherent worth—fosters trust. When we see others merely as participants in a group we often judge them too much on their ideas (which are good or bad), contributions (which are valuable or not), and role (which is a sliver of the total person). Coaching encourages people to listen deeper, investigate more thoroughly, and value others as people with a whole story being lived.

2. *Embracing conflict.* Out of trust is born healthy conflict, not absence of conflict. Just as individual coaching encourages the person being coached to sort through internal conflicts (choosing between options, deciding on best actions, determining when to say yes and when to say no), teams, to move forward, must be encouraged to engage in conflict. Teams often avoid conflict because an option, idea, or suggestion is tied too directly to the person who offered it. To reject an idea feels like the rejection of the person who offered it. Healthy teams are able to let ideas do battle because trust is present. When team members become known for more than their contributions to the team, others are able to separate people from their ideas and opinions. Coaching brings forth conflict: ideas, options, or actions held in contrast with one another so that the best can rise to the top. Coaching also keeps the conflict among the ideas, actions, and options rather than between people. Teams who utilize coaching welcome the tough conversations because the conflict serves a greater good.

3. *High commitment.* When ideas do battle (instead of people doing battle), the entire team is able to commit to the team's decisions because everyone has had opportunity to voice opinions. When people hold back (refuse to engage in the conflict), they inherently suffer low commitment. ("It wasn't really my idea, and I didn't think it was the best one, so I'm not fully bought in.") Coaching negotiates action by double- and triple-checking commitment. In a team environment, this is especially important. Coaching places high importance on nailing down not just the decision, but the level of commitment to the decision.

4. *Accountability.* High commitment enables teams to hold themselves accountable. Because everyone supports the decision (commitment), the team will want to celebrate the carrying out of the decision. This means team members will check back in and discuss what transpired after the decision without fear of seeming judgmental or heavy-handed. Since everyone supports the decision, each team member will welcome examination of any breakdown in carrying out the decision. The intentionality of coaching supports after-decision accountability: "Did we do what we agreed we would do?" Powerful questions and examination without blame are crucial for high-performance teams.

5. *Results.* Effective teams get results. Trust enables healthy conflict, which leads to strong commitment, which welcomes high accountability, which gets results. If results are not achieved, a team can be coached to see where the breakdown is by "peeling back the onion" of the other four characteristics. Coaching breeds an appreciation of results while avoiding worship of results. Coaching allows results to be appreciated without allowing results to attain a higher value than the persons who are performing to get the results. Because coaching is so highly relational, results are never in opposition to relationship. This

perspective frees teams of the task/relationship dichotomy that so often proves ineffective. For ministry teams, results equal ministry, so the appreciation of results has even higher importance.[10]

The Five Dysfunctions of a Team

Patrick Lencioni emphasizes that healthy and well-performing teams are the norm, not the exception. He then lists "five dysfunctions" that lead to poor performance: inattention to results, avoidance of accountability, lack of commitment, fear of conflict, and absence of trust.[11]

Third, coaching can help team leaders. Ministry team leaders often face a quandary of how to push a team (often composed of volunteers) forward to get things done without exercising executive authority. As one team leader stated, "How do I captain the team while being just another team member?" The tension of being coparticipant while leading is not uncommon to ministry teams. Leaders who integrate coaching into their team leadership will experience six rewards:

1. *Ability to foster productive conversation.* Teams that use a coach approach can create productive meetings. As various coaching conversation models demonstrate, a productive conversation (be it a team meeting or a discussion with one or more team members) has a particular flow. It begins by clarifying the topic of focus (What are we talking about?). It moves to gaining new understanding about the topic (What do we know? What challenges do we face? What opportunities exist? What options do we have?). It gets to commitment on what will happen next (What will we do as a result?). Team leaders who take a coach approach are catalysts for productive conversations that follow this flow. This flow supports the various models for a coaching conversation set forth in chapter 4.

2. *The power of focus.* Nearly every coaching conversation starts with a variant of the question, "How can we best use our time today?" The question immediately brings helpful parameters to the conversation and raises the value of certain topics. Effective ministry team leaders can use this coaching practice to bring focus to meetings, agendas, strategies, and plans. Such team leaders force the team to decide what's most important and then lead them to focus on only the most important. Studies show that teams with only two or three objectives have a high likelihood of accomplishing them. Teams with five to eight objectives will likely accomplish only two. Teams with ten objectives will likely

---

[10]Patrick Lencioni, *The Five Dysfunctions of a Team* (San Francisco: Jossey-Bass, 2002).
[11]Ibid.

accomplish one or none. Team leaders force choice to find focus: "What two things do we want to accomplish this year? What three agenda items can we cover in the next two hours? What one action will we take to move forward on this?"

3. *Guidance without imposed answers.* The genius of the coach approach to team leadership is that the leader is adept at pushing for decisions without having to personally make the decision. Coaches push the conversation forward but avoid making decisions on behalf of others. The same is true for ministry team leaders.

4. *Solicited participation from all team members.* People engage when they know where the conversation is going and know they can make a contribution. Using a coach approach ensures that every team member is tracking with and contributing to the conversation. In addition to waiting for people to participate, the coach approach encourages asking direct and powerful questions that solicit unique participation from each team member: "Don, you have a lot of experience with this kind of ministry. What do you think we might be missing?" "Judy, you seem to be deep in thought. What are you thinking?" "Carlos, you're a good left-brain logical thinker. Bring some balance to this heartfelt emotional conversation for the rest of us." "Tammy, you're one of our big-picture people. Help us see how this will affect other ministries in the church."

5. *High levels of ownership.* Team leaders succeed when the team, rather than the team leader, makes the decision, because whoever *makes* the decision *owns* the decision. Team members do not look to the leader to be the owner of the team's decisions, actions, or initiatives. Since coaching fully involves the team in decision-making—especially in committing to carrying out actions—the team leader can be certain that the team truly owns the action and will carry out the decisions made.

6. *Landing the plane.* Excitement and relief come from nailing things down and getting things accomplished. Coach approach team leaders do not let things hang in the air or remain fuzzy. They are masters at bringing clarity, focus, and closure. Rather than "talk things to death," they steer conversation toward birth of tangible decisions, actions, and commitments that bring hope and expectancy. They experience the reward of actually getting things done, both in meetings and in actual ministry.

■ ■ ■ The Leadership Team of Covenant Church invited a coach to facilitate their annual planning retreat. Before the meeting was turned over to the coach, Patty, the team leader, reviewed the minutes of the last meeting, thanked the secretary, Bruce, for taking such good notes, and double-checked to make sure Bruce would again record the proceedings of the current meeting.

Once the coach was asked to begin, she immediately reframed Bruce's role, asking that he only write down specific actions that would take place outside the team meeting. She then led the seven-member team to articulate what "success" for this meeting would look like. They decided the meeting would be a success if they determined the most important matters facing the church in the coming year and came up with a plan for addressing each of the important matters.

With that end in mind, she coached them to brainstorm the "important matters" and to focus on only two or three. This forced-choice experience helped the team get to the most important aspects of the most important matters. It also helped them allot their remaining three hours—giving one hour to each matter.

For each important matter, the coach asked questions to discover what were the current reality (X) and the desired reality (Y). She then led the team to brainstorm what actions could move the church forward from X to Y in the coming year and to settle on only two or three actions per matter. She helped them negotiate each action, refine it, remove any obstacles, establish a timeline, and assign someone from the team to be the champion for that action.

Near the end of the retreat, the coach asked Bruce to write all of the actions, totaling eight, on the dry erase board. She then asked the team members to assign a "commitment value" between one and ten to each action. The members wrote their numbers on color-specific cards. During a short break, the coach tabulated the average commitment value for each action. Surprisingly, two of the actions received average commitment values of less than seven, while the other six actions averaged at least nine. Based on this, the team decided to focus their energy on only the six actions to which they were highly committed.

Just as the retreat was ending, Bruce declared that a seventh "action" should be added: "Let's dedicate the majority of each team meeting this year to getting these six actions done with excellence." The rest of the team agreed. ■

Service to Those in Need

Coaching also provides skills and approach for doing ministry. This is true in at least two ways.

First, coaching affords Christians an effective way of discovering existing needs. Rather than assuming the needs of a given population, a coach approach assures a process of asking, listening, and being in dialogue. All great missionaries know this already. While all people need the truth and love of God through Jesus Christ, other needs also exist that can only be discovered by further exploration.

■ ■ ■ A rural church developed a desire to serve its surrounding community by meeting some practical needs in the name of Jesus. In a memorable brainstorming session, the leadership team discussed (guessed) what those needs might be: food for the poor? clothing for new-to-work mothers? Spanish classes for farm workers? After much debate, the team decided to *ask* the community, investing a series of Saturday mornings in conversations with their neighbors. The overwhelming response surprised church leaders. The community residents' top desire was a renewed sense of community. The area bordered three counties and was split among several school districts, ZIP codes, and telephone exchanges. The community did not feel like a community, but wanted to. The community was open to the church helping. ■

Second, coaching affords Christians an effective way of discovering how to meet existing needs. Christian coaches believe that all of the answers are within the person being coached according to the guidance of the Holy Spirit. This is largely true when it comes to servicing those in need, since persons being served often know (even when they don't think they know) what they need.

■ ■ ■ After the rural church (described above) discovered the biggest need was a stronger sense of community, church leaders asked and listened for how that need could best be met. Again, the answers surprised the church. While church leaders had considered community parties or other events as a good way to renew a sense of togetherness, neighbors had other ideas. Community residents said they wanted a convenience store and playground: places that provide a primary service (food, gas, recreation) and that offer a strong secondary impact (a sense of community). Residents felt little sense of community because they were not self-sufficient, having to drive some distance for provisions and recreation, and did not have places to gather and meet one another in the course of everyday activities. They did not want special events; they wanted ordinary opportunities for community. Church leaders would have never known this had they not suspended judgment, asked some powerful questions, and listened intently to the replies. ■

Witness to Those Who Do Not Know God: A Coach Approach to Evangelism

A single word can carry many different meanings for many different people. One such word is *evangelism.*

Even in Christian circles, the word *evangelism* gets assigned simultaneous and distinct meanings. For some, the word indicates the sharing of Christ's good news, plain and simple. For others, the word has negative connotations of smooth-talking hucksters trying to connive people into making a decision. For others, the word indicates a set of skills or an approach to life that invites people into relationship with Christ. The word is even used in non-church settings to indicate what might best be understood as word-of-mouth marketing.

Evangelism for Today's Condition

The dissonance around *evangelism* likely stems more from how to go about evangelizing than from lack of understanding about what it is. The old definitions still fit; believers are called to be used by God to help others find life in Jesus. However, as North America becomes a missional setting for ministry, the evangelism strategies of our revivalist era grow more and more out of step. The days of "proclaiming in an effort to persuade" may need to give way to more effective strategies that fit the mindset and mood of today's would-be followers of Christ.

Today disconnectedness from God and one another is experienced less as a sense of guilt and more as a sense of shame. Whereas a sense of guilt can be removed via pardon, shame requires the person to narrate a new story for themselves, a process that takes time and constant attention.[12] Space here does not allow for elaboration, but suffice it to say that today's context calls for evangelistic approaches that are marked by process and by narrative. Coaching can serve as one of these new approaches to evangelism.

How does coaching find a place in today's evangelism context? Put plainly, the story coaching tells is quite similar to the "grand narrative" of our faith: Humans are not what they should be. Helpful relationships can move people toward their potential by helping them live lives aligned to truth, which produces real results and better lives.

But where does Jesus come into all of this? When people become acquainted with coaching, one common misconception is that "all of the resources for a whole life lie within the person." If this were true, everyone could be their own "savior," and no one would need Jesus, except perhaps to serve as teacher or as role model.

Effective coaching helps a person benefit from both internal and external solutions. Coaches guide a person in discovering internal resources as well as what is missing. The key is that the coach (unlike a consultant or counselor) does not tell the person what is missing. The coach converses with the person to elicit discovery of what is missing and what is needed. When it comes to living a truly abundant life, every human needs a Savior who can usher the person out of a story of shame and isolation and into a

---

[12]See Alan Mann, *Atonement for a "Sinless" Society* (Waynesboro, Ga.: Paternoster, 2005).

story of hope and connection. A coach approach to evangelism can facilitate this discovery and open a person to the saving influence of Jesus.

Evangelists who want to take a coach approach can use four coaching practices that are found in the life of Christ.

1. *Start with an attitude of humility.* Although believers know each person needs Christ's saving work, much about another person remains unknown. Christ rarely started with a person's "large-scale spiritual condition of disconnectedness." Rather, He started with the felt reality of that condition—a woman caught in adultery, a tax collector whose chosen profession had created a life of isolation, or a rich young man who wondered what more there was to life than living obediently according to the Temple laws. Jesus started with where people found themselves. A coach approach to evangelism begins with believers humbly admitting that they cannot tell people where they are or what they need. Believers must engage people in humble dialogues of discovery.

2. *Be patient with the process.* Coaching does not offer a quick-fix set of principles that can be easily applied to create a more effective life. Instead, coaching is a relational process. This relationship has a unique spiral-like rhythm that might be described as "discovery and alignment." As applied to evangelism, this unique rhythmic process helps a person engage Christ over time and shift attitudes and behaviors along the way. Rather than one fell swoop, following Christ is an ever-deepening process. This means the lines between evangelism and discipleship will necessarily blur. Christ engaged the disciples for three years, constantly helping them discover new layers of truth and live into what they had discovered. Their early commitment to "follow" initiated a slow process of coming to saving faith. Evangelism coaches will need to nudge the process along and not grow impatient with people who seem reluctant to express a fully mature faith commitment.

3. *Ask lots of questions.* Evangelism coaches will want to get curious about people and help them move forward by offering potent questions that draw people into discovering what is true.

Sample Questions
- What's going on in your life right now?
- In what ways have you challenged that (false) belief?
- Who are your role models?
- What is bringing the most life to your life right now?
- If you were able to make one significant change to improve your life right now, what would it be?
- What books are you reading right now? What are they telling you about how to live life?

- Where do you think most of your beliefs come from?
- What's your opinion of Jesus?
- When you pray, what do you pray for?

These kinds of questions can open the conversation to explore spiritual topics, including the other person's relationship to God.

---

4. *Identify meaningful actions.* For a couple of hundred years, evangelism has focused on getting someone to agree to a principle and to express this mental assent in a prayer. Surprisingly, Jesus never led anyone in what many call the sinner's prayer or talked about "the four spiritual laws" that tracts today outline. His tactic was to push for meaningful actions that expressed and deepened the mental assent. If you love me, feed my sheep (Jn. 6:57). If you believe love is more powerful than violence, then turn the other cheek, offer the shirt off your back, and propose to go the second mile (Mt. 5:39–41). If you want to be a part of my way of life, find a partner, and go cast out demons and heal diseased people (Mk. 16:17–18). Evangelism coaches will help people go beyond prayer by finding the next best action that lives out transformational truth.

Since today's would-be followers of Christ need an evangelism approach that helps people move forward in a process of discovering their deep need for Christ, it's easy to see how coaching fits the bill. An evangelism coach enters into an enduring relationship with someone to help that person re-narrate life according to truth that is discovered and Truth *who* is discovered (Christ). Evangelism coaching places the starting point of the evangelism process with the person's current felt condition. Coaching helps a person open up to reveal what is missing and what is needed to make the story complete and the life whole. By using the skills and habits of a coach, followers of Christ can be used by God to guide people into salvation.

This chapter has focused on opportunities to use coaching in a congregational setting. Coaching can also have a powerful and positive impact on other ministries. For more information, see appendix 4, "Ministries That Thrive with Coaching" (p.142).

A Prayer for Congregations Using Coaching

God, what a gift You have given us in relationship. You have created us for relationship. You are fighting our state of disconnectedness and restoring us to relationship with You and with one another. And You are winning.

May we follow Your lead and commit ourselves to the mission of restoration. And may we engage in this struggle relationally. Thank You for the gift of coaching, as it provides a powerful way of relating and of restoring relationship.

For those who lead others to worship You, we pray they will have Your glory as their chief aim. We know that the only way to approach You is with a humble heart, in an attitude of thankfulness, and through the power of Christ. May pastors, preachers, proclaimers, and other worship leaders robe themselves in Christ and approach You in worship.

For those who serve as catalysts for community, please be their Provider. As they gaze upon Your threefold nature, give them glimpses of what true relationship looks like. Let them not be lonely in their work.

For those whose hearts beat for the mission of connecting others to You, encourage them as they work through the many roadblocks that would detour them to less important matters.

In Christ the Great Connector's name we pray, Amen.

Beyond the Book

- Following worship this week, ask a friend or family member a powerful question based on the message or another aspect of the worship service.
- What other endeavors, ministries, or programs can you think of that would benefit from a coach approach?
- Who is one person (or group) you can serve this month? When can you coach them to discover a need you could help meet? What will be your first question?
- With whom is Christ calling you into deeper community? If you were to double your listening with this person, where might your relationship be in one year? What specific steps will you take to deepen that relationship?
- Who is one person in your church or community that you can coach forward in a spiritual journey? When will you ask that person to enter into a coaching relationship with you? How will you ask?

AFTERWORD

Jesus as Our Master Coach

Early in this book, we introduced you to a working definition: *Christian coaching is a focused Christ-centered relationship that cultivates a person's sustained growth and action.* By this definition, Jesus truly was a Master Coach.

This is not to say that Jesus and coaching are synonymous. We do not want to overstate the importance of coaching or speak in gross hyperbole. Jesus did much more than coach. He mentored. He taught. He healed. He atoned for our sins. After all, the world needed a Savior, not a coach. But while Jesus and coaching are not synonymous, we can fix our eyes upon strong similarities between the two.

Think about it! Jesus invested three years in relationship with a handful of men and women to inaugurate, in a special way, God's kingdom. Each of His relationships was totally Christ-centered, not because of His ego or dysfunction, but because He knew Himself to be the Way, the Truth, and the Life (Jn. 14:6). He spent time drawing people to Himself so they could find the abundance of a relationship with God through Him (Jn. 10:10b).

Jesus entered into relationships so that something would happen. The relationships Jesus fostered cultivated sustained growth and action. Those who encountered Jesus grew in so many ways: knowledge, willingness, submission, faith, and passion. These men and women also became persons of action, so much so that the fifth book of the New Testament has become known as the Acts of the Apostles. The growth and action of those first followers resulted in a sustained unfolding of God's plan for His world. As Jesus said, even the powers of hell cannot stop it (Mt. 16:18).

Jesus still is a Master Coach. He longs to listen to you and to ask you precise questions; He wants to deliver direct messages to you and to aid you in identifying meaningful actions. He wants to coach you to make Him Lord and Savior of your life and to let that be the starting line (not the finish line!) for a life of faithfulness. A life of faithfulness includes covenanting with Jesus to allow Him to coach you in life's ups and downs, toward life's ultimate answers, and throughout your entire life. He wants a relationship with you that cultivates your sustained growth and action.

Prayerfully consider now how Jesus is leading you in exploring your pathway as a coach. Many options are available. Consider appendix 3, "Developing Your Pathway as a Coach" (p. 137), for ideas and guidance.

A Closing Prayer

We pray that all who read this book will find Jesus to be their Master Coach. Lord, walk alongside them, being the Paraclete who aids them in seeing clearly who You intend them to be and what You intend them to do.

Take the lessons from this book and breathe on them to create holy growth and meaningful action in the lives of the readers. Give them eyes to see the coaching path that You have set before them, give them heart to commit to walking the path, and give them ears to hear Your words of encouragement as they journey forward.

In Jesus' name we pray. Amen.

APPENDIX ONE

Distinctions of Coaching

How Is Coaching Distinct from Other Service Professions?

Professional coaching is a distinct service that focuses on an individual's life as it relates to goal setting, outcome creation, and personal change management. To understand what a coach is, you may find it helpful to distinguish coaching from other professions that provide personal or organizational support.

Therapy

Coaching can be distinguished from therapy in a number of ways. First, coaching is a profession that supports personal and professional growth and development based on individual-initiated change in pursuit of specific actionable outcomes. These outcomes are linked to personal or professional success.

Second, coaching is forward moving and future focused. Therapy, on the other hand, deals with healing pain, dysfunction, and conflict within an individual or in a relationship between two or more individuals. The focus is often on resolving difficulties arising from the past—which hamper an individual's emotional functioning in the present—improving overall psychological functioning, and dealing with present life and work circumstances in more emotionally healthy ways. Therapy outcomes often include improved emotional/feeling states. While positive feelings/emotions may be a natural outcome of coaching, the primary focus is on creating actionable strategies for achieving specific goals in one's work or personal life. The emphasis in a coaching relationship is on action, accountability, and follow through.

Consulting

Consultants may be retained by individuals or organizations for the purpose of accessing specialized expertise. While consulting approaches vary widely, people often assume that the consultant diagnoses problems and prescribes and sometimes implements solutions. In general, the assumption with coaching is that individuals or teams are capable of generating their own solutions, with the coach supplying supportive, discovery-based approaches and frameworks.

Mentoring

Mentoring can be thought of as guiding from one's own experience or sharing of experience in a specific area of industry or career development and is sometimes confused with coaching. Mentoring develops skills and instills wisdom based on the mentor's life. Although some coaches provide mentoring as part of their coaching, such as in "mentor coaching" new coaches, coaches are not typically mentors to those they coach.

Training

Training programs are based on the acquisition of certain learning objectives as set out by the trainer or instructor. Though objectives are clarified in the coaching process, they are set by the individual or team being coached, with the coach providing guidance. Training also assumes a linear learning path that coincides with an established curriculum. Coaching is less linear and without a set curriculum plan.

Athletic Development

Though non-sport coaches often use sports metaphors, they are differ-ent from the traditional sports coach. The athletic coach is often seen as an expert who guides and directs the behavior of individuals or teams based on his or her greater experience and knowledge. Non-sport coaches possess these qualities, but it is the experience and knowledge of the individual or team that determines the direction. Additionally, non-sport coaching, unlike athletic development, does not focus on behaviors that are being executed poorly or incorrectly. Instead, the focus is on identifying opportunity for development based on individual strengths and capabilities.

Material in this appendix is used with permission by the International Coach Federation, www.coachfederation.org.

APPENDIX TWO

Sample Coaching Documents

Sample 1: A Coaching Agreement Covenant

Coaching Agreement

Name:_____Phone:_____

Address:_____

Call Procedure

You and your coach are scheduled to talk once a week for thirty minutes each session. You will receive eight sessions total. Your coach will initiate the call, so please be available at the specified time each week. Please remember that this time has been reserved for you and respect it. If a change is needed, please give your coach twenty-four–hours notice to reschedule a session. Without proper notice, missed coaching calls will be lost. Your coach requests that you make your time together a priority.

Problems

If your coach says or does anything that upsets you or does not feel right, please bring it to his/her attention. Honesty and trust are critical for the relationship to grow.

Please read the following, and sign and date on the lines below:

As a client, I understand and agree that I am fully responsible for my well-being during my coaching calls, including my choices and my decisions. I am aware that I can choose to discontinue coaching at any time. I also recognize that coaching is not therapy and that professional referrals will be given to me if needed.

Client: _____Date: _____

Coach: _____Date: _____

See Coach U's Essential Coaching Tools book (full resource information listed in appendix 5) for more practical documents for use with clients. A CD-ROM is included with Coach U's book.

Sample 2: A Sample Coaching Agreement

Coaching Agreement

Name:_____

Address: _____

Phone:_____Fax: _____E-mail: _____

Initial Term:_____Fee:_____

Day/Time of Call:_____Length of Call: _____

Call Procedure: _____

Services Provided: _____

_____

_____

Focus of Work: _____

_____

_____

Ground Rules: 1. Calls are on time. 2. Client pays for long distance.

_____

Please read the following and sign and date on the lines below:

As a client, I understand and agree that I am fully responsible for my well-being during my coaching calls, including my choices and my decisions. I am aware that I can choose to discontinue coaching at any time. I also recognize that coaching is not therapy and that professional referrals will be given to me if needed.

Client: _____Date: _____

Coach: _____Date: _____

Sample 3: A Sample Coaching Agreement/Covenant

Coaching Agreement

Christian coaching is an ongoing relationship between a coach and a person who desires/wants coaching. We agree that:

1. Coaching is not therapy, counseling, advice-giving, mental health care, or treatment for substance abuse. The coach is not functioning as a licensed mental health professional, and coaching is not intended as a replacement for counseling, psychiatric interventions, treatment for mental illness, recovery from past abuse, professional medical advice, financial assistance, legal counsel, or other professional services.
2. Coaching is for people who are basically well-adjusted, emotionally healthy, functioning effectively, and want to make changes in their lives.
3. Coaching is designed to address issues the person being coached would like to consider. These could include (but are not limited to) career development, relationship enhancement, spiritual growth, lifestyle management, life balance, decision-making, and achieving short-term or long-term goals. For our coaching relationship, we have agreed to limit the focus to issues that are related to your role in leading congregational redevelopment.
4. Coaching will be an ongoing relationship that may take a number of months, although either party can terminate the relationship at any time. Some or all coaching may be through telephone contact.
5. Coaching can involve brainstorming, values clarification, the completion of written assignments, education, goal setting, identifying plans of action, accountability, making requests, agreements to change behavior, examining lifestyles, and questioning.
6. Coaching is most effective when both parties are honest and straightforward in their communications.
7. If the coaching is to involve payment for services, prior to its beginning both parties will agree to a fee, form of payment, procedures for cancelled appointments, and initial length of commitment.
8. Coaching is a confidential relationship, and the coach agrees to keep all information strictly confidential, except in those situations where such confidentiality would violate the law.
9. Coaching assumes that each person in the relationship is guided by his or her values and beliefs. As a Christian coach, I am a committed follower of Jesus Christ and seek to live in accordance with this commitment. The Christian coach is honest in making this revelation, but he or she respects the different values and beliefs of others. The Christian coach does not seek to impose his or her values on another, proselytize, condemn, or refuse coaching services to people who do not share similar values and beliefs.
10. Each of the people whose signatures appear below agrees that this agreement represents our mutual understanding of the coaching relationship.

Person Being Coached:_____Date_____
(Signature)

Coach:_____Date_____
(Signature)

Sample 4: A Sample Welcome Letter and Covenant

Welcome!

I am delighted to be your coach and look forward to coaching you toward creating the changes and life you really want and are designed to have. To get us started, I have some policies and procedures I want to familiarize you with. Please, if you have any questions regarding these, we can freely discuss them further.

Commitment

You are contracting with me as your coach because you want to make significant change in your life. Because change happens over time, I am requesting a six-session commitment (up to two hours of coaching per month) to the coaching process. This allows the coaching relationship to develop and begin to be powerful.

The cost for this service is $_____ a session for six sessions, payable in advance. Payments should be made to "_____" and mailed to the address in the header of this page. Full or partial refunds are available should you decide the coaching relationship is not meeting your needs.

After the initial six sessions, we can renegotiate the agreement to continue, if desired.

Coaching Sessions

The coaching will be conducted on dates and at times that fit your schedule. This will entitle you up to two hours of coaching per month. Typically, each coaching session will be scheduled on an every-other-week or every-third-week basis. Each coaching session is typically scheduled for fifty-five minutes.

Calling Procedure

You will call me at _____ at your scheduled appointment time. This is my coaching line that will forward to me wherever I may be.

Confidentiality

All information discussed and/or shared during coaching sessions will be kept strictly confidential (unless otherwise required by law). At times, information that is shared may be specific and explicitly personal. Your willingness to be truthful will be treated with ultimate respect; this is a special confidence.

Coaching Relationship

The service I provide to you is tele-coaching designed jointly with you. Coaching is not advice, therapy, or counseling. It may address specific personal projects, life balance, career successes, or general conditions in your life or profession.

Throughout our coaching relationship, the conversations will continue to be direct and personal. You can count on me to be honest and straightforward, asking clarifying questions and making empowering requests. The purpose of our interaction is to hold your focus on your desired outcome and coach you to stay clear, focused, and in action. You understand that the power of the coaching relationship can only be granted by you, and you agree to do just that: grant that the coaching relationship be powerful.

If you see that coaching is not working as desired or if I ever say or do something that upsets you or doesn't feel right, please bring it to my attention on the call. I promise to do what is necessary to have you be satisfied.

Changes

Rescheduling an appointment is easy with advanced twenty-four–hour notice. If you have an emergency, we'll work around it.

E-mail

Communications, homework accountability, and more can be handled through e-mail. Your monthly fee entitles you to e-mail me and anticipate a response within forty-eight hours. Use e-mail frequently to stay in touch.

Sample 5: For Use by a Coaching Client in Preparation for a Coaching Session

Prep Form for Coaching Client

Get the most out of your coaching call by preparing for it!

Date _____

What I have accomplished since our last call

What I didn't get done, but intended to

The challenges and problems I am facing now

The opportunities that are available to me right now

I want to use the coach during the call to

What I promise to do by the next call

Sample 6: For Use by a Coaching Client in Preparing for a Coaching Session

Coaching Client's Preparation Form

Date_____

What key learnings did I have this week?

What am I most proud of this week?

How did I let myself down this week?

What commitments will I make to go forward?

What support is needed?

Sample 7: For Use by Coaching Clients in Identifying What Might Be Holding Them Back

What Am I Tolerating?

We humans certainly have learned to tolerate a lot! We put up with, take on, and are dragged down by other people's behavior, situations, unmet needs, crossed boundaries, incompletions, frustrations, problems, and even our own behavior. You are tolerating more than you think. So what are you tolerating?

Please take a couple of minutes to write down ten things you might be tolerating. Do you have to do anything about these? No, not really. Just becoming aware of and articulating them will bring them to the forefront of your soul. You'll then naturally start handling, eliminating, fixing, growing through, and resolving these tolerations. Enjoy this exercise, okay?

1. _____

2. _____

3. _____

4. _____

5. _____

6. _____

7. _____

8. _____

9. _____

10. _____

See Coach U's Essential Coaching Tools Book *for more practical documents for use with clients. CD-ROM included with the book.*

Sample 8: For Use by a Coaching Client in Preparation for a Coaching Relationship

Action Plan

Use this page to identify four of your goals as well as the five action steps to reach each goal. Be brief and specific. Choose only actions that directly support your goal. Once you've reached the goals, set new ones as needed.

Goal 1 _____

    Action 1 _____

    Action 2 _____

    Action 3 _____

    Action 4 _____

    Action 5 _____

Goal 2 _____

    Action 1 _____

    Action 2 _____

    Action 3 _____

    Action 4 _____

    Action 5 _____

Goal 3 _____

    Action 1 _____

    Action 2 _____

    Action 3 _____

    Action 4 _____

    Action 5 _____

Goal 4 _____

    Action 1 _____

    Action 2 _____

    Action 3 _____

    Action 4 _____

    Action 5 _____

Sample 9: A Sample Description of Coaching and Benefits for Use by a Coach in Educating/Preparing the Client

Coaching Information

Coaching has proven to have very powerful results when a person is ready to learn more about him/herself and his/her relationships with others. Coaching offers a combination of deepening learning about negotiating and reacting to the environment and forwarding action toward making long-term behavior changes. People find that once they clearly understand where they are today and where they want to be, closing that gap will enable them to enhance interpersonal effectiveness, make a career or personal change, improve their business results, and/or create a more satisfying and successful life.

The Coaching Relationship allows you to:

1. *Take more, better, and smarter actions.* You create the vision and goals you want. Our initial work together will focus on identifying what you want and who you need to be to lead change in your congregation. This is different from what you "could, should, ought to, and have to do." When you can envision your desired future, you will naturally and consistently make choices that honor your values and move you toward your goals.

2. *Stretch yourself.* You will find yourself stretching out of your comfort zone and experiencing growth in the areas of discomfort. If you were already where you wanted to be and were who you needed to be, you would have the success you desire to have. This coaching relationship will seek to stretch you into becoming the person who leads the redevelopment journey and helps your entire congregation close the gap between where they currently are and where God wants them to be.

3. *Use the power of language to enhance your effectiveness.* Looking at the words you use in everyday conversations provides insight into how your and others' experiences might be deleted, distorted, and/or generalized. We'll explore areas in which language holds you back and find more effective language that supports and serves you as you seek to create a climate of change and positive passion.

4. *Make better decisions.* As your coach, I am fully committed to supporting your overall agenda and the agenda you bring to each of our conversations. To that end, my role is to be vigilant in ensuring your decisions are in service of what you want to achieve or accomplish. I will "hold" your agenda and provide accountability that your decisions are moving you toward fulfillment of your agenda.

5. *Have more sustainable energy.* When you are living in the present and not tangled in the past or caught up in what could or might happen in the future, your energy is focused, productive, and free of tolerations and problems. The weight of "what to do" is a powerful sedative. A natural drain saps your energy as you try to fight through the cloud of confusion that comes from being trapped in the moment. Coaching helps you "move to the balcony" and look down on your situation from a vantage point that is free from the tangles of your context.

APPENDIX THREE

Developing Your Pathway
as a Coach

One of our favorite coaching axioms is "there is no coaching without action." Throughout this book, we have encouraged you to go "beyond the book," to take coaching into your world and allow this new approach to impact the way you relate to yourself and those around you. We now encourage you to consider your pathway as a coach and the long-lasting impact of coaching on your ministry and life.

We do not expect everyone who reads this book to drop their careers and become full-time coaches. In fact, we expect such a scenario to be the exception. Instead, we anticipate the best impact of this work will be for you, the reader, to discover the unique expression of coaching in your life and to live into that expression. To facilitate the discovery and expression of coaching in your life, we offer the following "potential pathways." These are not well-paved highways with few off-ramps, but paths that we have noticed others taking and that may lead you to discover your own path. Moving forward in coaching is not like cutting a new path through thick underbrush, but more like hiking through fields and forests where stamina is required but the landscape is open for exploration and enjoyment.

For Those Who Want to Use Coaching Skills from Time to Time:
- Reread the coaching skills chapters and locate the skill(s) that appeal most to you and those that you can most readily apply in your setting.
- Consider picking a skill that you don't generally use and bring it into conversations.
- Consider how coaching might positively impact various aspects of your life, such as vocation, volunteer, family, and community.
- Focus on one or two relationships, and intentionally use coaching skills with those people. Notice what happens.
- Look for articles or books that will stretch your knowledge of coaching to increase your understanding.
- Ask for feedback from those around you (peers, family, coworkers) about how you are currently living out the skill(s) and what potential positive outcomes could result from your increasing your proficiency in using the skill(s).
- Hire a coach to help you grow personally as you use coaching with others.
- Ask: "What could life look like if I employed this skill set well?"

For Those Who Want to Use Coaching Informally in Their Current Ministry (or Work-related) Role:

- Identify two or three current relationships in which you can intentionally coach. Notice what happens!
- Review the International Coach Federation's Coaching Competencies, available online at www.coachfederation.org. Choose several competencies, and write a statement of what each competency would look like in your current role.
- Seek out a mentor coach, someone who is using coaching in a similar role.

For Those Who Want to Use Coaching Formally in Their Current Ministry (or Work–related) Role:

- Ask: "When it comes to my current job description, what needs to be added to include coaching and what needs to be taken away?"
- Ask: "How can I change my current role, my job, or my career to get into more of a coaching role?"
- Seek out coaching "clients" from within your current organization or beyond. Get as much coaching experience as possible to continue your growth as a coach.
- Go to www.coachfederation.org, the International Coach Federation Web site. Look at the requirements and guidelines for certification, and explore how seeking coach certification could benefit your growth and ability as a coach right now.
- If you are considering hiring a coach, be diligent in asking the coach if he or she has been specifically trained in coaching skills and currently holds or is in the process of acquiring an ICF credential. Don't be misled to think a coach is competent because of other professional credentials or high fees.
- Track your coaching hours (from the very beginning!) so they can be counted toward ICF certification requirements. Check the ICF Web site for details on what needs to be tracked.
- Explore training options. Consider coaching workshops that incorporate hands-on training that will allow you to practice coaching as a part of the training. The authors of this book offer training through Valwood Christian Leadership Coaching, The Columbia Partnership, and Western Seminary. Appendix 5, "Resources for Coaching" (p. 145), has information on each of these as well as other training options.
- Compare training options from Christian and from secular sources to find those that will best fit your needs.
- Develop a short "elevator speech" describing what coaching is and inviting persons to be coached by you.
- Develop a coaching agreement or covenant that can be used to create a formal coaching relationship. Appendix 2, "Sample Coaching

Documents" (p. 127), and *Coach U's Essential Coaching Tools* (see p. 145) have excellent examples to get you started in crafting an agreement.

• Hire a coach, and work on strengthening any areas that need to be shored up in your life. Focusing on yourself in your coaching is a great way to "walk the talk."

For Those Who Want to Become a "Full-Time Coach":

• Review the International Coaching Federation's guidelines for certification and seek out a training program that follows ICF's competencies.
• Hire a coach who can serve as a mentor coach in helping you fully live into your role as a coach.
• Be certain to track your hours for ICF certification. Check the ICF Web site for details on what needs to be tracked.
• Consider whether you want to make a leap into coaching full time, take some big steps that will lead to coaching full time, or slowly migrate toward coaching full time, and plan accordingly.

Hiring a Coach

Whatever your pathway, we strongly encourage you to find a coach. There is no better way to learn about coaching or learn how to coach than to be coached by a skilled and experienced coach. James S. Vuocolo offers some helpful hints for finding and hiring a coach.[1]

Four Steps to Finding the Right Coach:

1. *Be clear about what you want.* A good coach is going to ask what it is that you want. While it may seem elementary, not everyone knows the answer to this question! Most people are not used to being asked what they want in life or in work. If it helps, start by listing all the things you know you do not want; and go from there! People hire coaches either because they want more of something and less of something else or because they are facing a personal or professional dilemma. Still others see something in the coach that attracts them, whether they can articulate what that may be, or not. The job of a coach is to model a great life!

2. *Understand that coaching is all about you!* Coaching is about you–your life, your work, your goals, your needs, your desires, your dreams, your values, etc. Coaching is not about the coach's life, work goals, needs, desires, dreams, values, etc. This is your time and your space– and a trained and qualified coach is going to make this all about you! I like to think of it as offering my clients a sacred space wherein they

---

[1]Information from James Vuocolo can be found online at www.newsday.com/media/acrobat/2007-01/27265876.pdf.

can come to share any and every thing on their minds and hearts. And, like a fitting room, they can try on new ideas like trying on a new suit of clothing—without fear of recrimination, competition, or rejection.

3. *Interview more than one coach, and have your own list of questions ready.* The most important thing to look for in selecting a coach is finding someone with whom you feel you can easily relate to create the most powerful partnership possible. Here are some questions you may want to ask prospective coaches: What is your coaching experience? (number of individuals you have coached, years of experience, types of situations, etc.) What is your coach-specific training? Do you hold an ICF, IAC, or WABC credential? Are you enrolled in an ICF accredited training program? What is your coaching specialty or client areas you most often work in? What specialized skills or experience do you bring to your coaching? What is your philosophy about coaching? What is your specific process for coaching? (How sessions are conducted, frequency, etc.) What are some coaching success stories? (Ask for specific examples of individuals who have done well and examples of how you have added value.) What's the average length of time you work with clients who are addressing situations similar to my own? What are your fees, and how are they normally paid?

4. *When you're ready to retain the personal or business coach that you've selected, be ready to do some work!* Most coaches will have you read over and sign a "Coaching Agreement" form that outlines the specifics you both have agreed upon with regard to the number and length of sessions per month, the initial duration of the coaching agreement, the agreed upon fee, etc. You may also be asked to sign a credit card authorization form to make convenient payments. Many coaches also have a series of documents they call a "Welcome Pak," or the equivalent. These documents are designed to assist the coach to learn a lot about you quickly, as well as assisting you to work through some things that will enable you to be clear about your priorities, long- and short-range goals, and more.

Additionally, Jane Creswell has offered the following:

Tips for Finding a Christ-centered Coach[2]:

* Get biographical information for at least three coaches.

* Pay close attention to: coach certification (and the certifying organization)—ICF certification is the international standard for professionalism and ethics in coaching—coach training; coaching experience; Christian confession and involvement; references.

---

[2]Jane Creswell, *Christ-Centered Coaching: 7 Benefits for Ministry Leaders* (St. Louis: Chalice Press, 2006) 143–44.

✳ Ask for a sample coaching session. Pay attention to how well you connect and whether you think you could quickly build a trusting relationship. Note if the coach speaks readily of God and of personal faith.

✳ Creswell's tips about where to find a coach include:
- www.coachfederation.org
- www.thecolumbiapartnership.org
- www.valwoodcoaching.com
- www.westerncoaches.net
- www.christiancoaches.com

Note: The above is not an exhaustive list of where to find a Christian coach. Ask others for recommendations.

Whether you decide to become a full time coach or to just use coaching informally, enjoy every moment of the journey! Coaching is a wonderful adventure, both for you and for those around you!

ICF recognizes three levels of coach credentials. We have briefly outlined the differences below and the basic requirements for each level as of time of printing:

Associate Certified Coach (ACC)

60 hours of coach-specific training
100 hours of coaching experience with clients
Satisfactory completion of oral exam
Agreement to adhere to the Code of Ethics as outlined by the ICF

Professional Certified Coach (PCC)

125 hours of coach-specific training
750 hours of coaching experience with clients
Satisfactory completion of written and oral exam
Agreement to adhere to the Code of Ethics as outlined by the ICF
Continued professional development to renew credential every three years

Master Certified Coach (MCC)

200 hours of coach-specific training
2,500 hours of coaching experience with clients
Satisfactory completion of written and oral exam
Demonstrated leadership within the profession
Agreement to adhere to the Code of Ethics as outlined by the ICF
Continued professional development to renew credential every three years

APPENDIX FOUR

Ministries That Thrive with Coaching

Coaching is a powerful way of relating that can have a positive impact for the kingdom of God. This book has highlighted ways coaching can be used on a personal level (by and for Christian leaders) and on the congregational level (for worship, community, and service). These conversations have in no way been exhaustive. Perhaps they have sparked your imagination for exploring coaching in your ministry context. This appendix will highlight other ways that coaching can be used in ministry settings to support the church's mission and may also spark your own ideas for using coaching.

	DENOMINATIONS
Context That Invites Coaching	• Churches from the same denomination may conduct widely different programs. For example, in the arena of Christian education/formation, churches from the same denomination might offer ministries as diverse as Sunday school, small groups, university-type courses conducted on a semester system, home churches, cell churches, and more. The same is true for outreach, stewardship, children's, and pastoral care programs.
	• Churches from the same denomination may vary in how they conduct the same program. For example, a children's Sunday school program might use rotating teachers, learning labs, a traditional curriculum approach, a large group celebration, or self-published materials. The same condition is similarly true for worship services. The expressions of a particular program are so diverse that it becomes impossible for a denomination to even keep up.
	• The rise of the teaching church has had a decentralizing effect on expertise and advice. Many churches no longer turn first to their denomination or even to a teaching church from within their denomination.
	• Barriers between denominations are beginning to break down. Cross-denominational pollination is becoming the norm. Many churches are finding they may have much in common even though they are from different denominations. This is heightened by the rise of successful non-denominational congregations as well as congregations that deemphasize their denomination.

Current Coaching Reality—How Denominations Are Utilizing Coaching	• *In service to leaders.* Denominations are offering coaching services to church and judicatory leaders. This takes various forms: ongoing coaching for a leader, coaching for a planning or staff meeting, coaching for a staff around a particular issue.
	• *Coaching for church planters.*
	• *In service to congregations.* Denominations are offering coaching and coach-oriented services to assist entire congregations in moving forward.
	• *Internal.* Denominations are offering coaching services to their own staff to improve performance and maintain balance.
	• *In conjunction with training.* Denominations are offering coaching to workshop and conference participants to help them put new learnings into action.
	• *Training for coaches.* Denominations are setting up coach training opportunities for ministry leaders who can benefit from taking a coach approach to ministry.
	PARACHURCH
Context That Invites Coaching	• Most parachurch ministries focus their efforts on one aspect of the church's work (discipleship, evangelism, missions, service to the poor, etc.), meaning they face the same "one size does not fit all" reality in which coaching thrives.
	• Decentralized staff are asked to achieve similar outcomes in widely differing settings. Managers of such staff have to find ways to bring out the best in their staff while allowing for unique approaches that will work in a given context.
	• Ministry on the margins involves people who do not buy into typical church programming or incentives, but are open to tailored approaches for growth and ministry.
	• Cross-cultural ministries (age, gender, race, religion, background, socio-economic, etc.) face barriers when it comes to importing what works for one people group for use with another people group.
Current Coaching Reality	• Coaching of church planters who are supported by parachurch and missions agencies rather than a denomination.
	• Coaching of believers who were formerly a part of a campus ministry.
	• Coaching for missionaries and mission support staff.
	• Coaching on mission field for translating ministry into more indigenous forms.
	• Post-training coaching for staff to help translate new learnings into improved performance.

- Example: Lead Like Jesus is an organization that offers coaching to persons who want to implement that organization's principles.
- Example: World Vision is an organization that offers coaching for leaders on a global context.

	EDUCATION
Context That Invites Coaching	• Heightened appreciation of adult-learning principles results in seminaries needing to take an andragogy approach rather than pedagogy, opening the door to a coach approach to learning and training. • Widely heterogeneous ministry context negates a homogenous approach to ministry preparation. • The uncertain and unpredictable nature of today's congregational life means ministers need training that prepares them to be flexible and discovery-minded.
Current Coaching Reality	• Schools adapting coaching principles into their teaching approaches. • Coaching being offered as a part of doctor of ministry programs to give pastors new skills for dealing with parishioners who do not need counseling, as well as for dealing with staff and teams. • Coaching courses offered in master of divinity and master of arts programs. • Coaching being offered to students as they enter their degree programs and as they leave their degree programs. • Example: Western Seminary in Portland, Oregon, offers eight coaching courses as well as mentor coaching for students.

APPENDIX FIVE

Resources for Coaching

Books

Bacon, Terry and Karen Spear. *Adaptive Coaching.* Palo Alto, Calif.: Davies Black Publishing, 2003.

Berman-Fortgang, Laura. *Now What: 90 Days to a New Life Direction.* New York: Penguin Group, 2004.

Blanchard, Scott and Madeleine Homan. *Leverage Your Best, Ditch the Rest.* New York: HarperCollins, 2004.

Borg, Marcus. *The Heart of Christianity: Rediscovering a Life of Faith.* New York: HarperCollins, 2003.

Buckingham, Marcus. *The One Thing You Need to Know About Great Managing, Great Leadership, and Sustained Individual Success.* New York: Free Press, 2005.

Bullard, George. *Pursuing the Full Kingdom Potential of Your Congregation.* St. Louis: Lake Hickory Press, 2005.

Coach U. *Coach U's Essential Coaching Tools.* Hoboken, N.J.: John Wiley and Sons, 2005.

Collins, Gary. *Christian Coaching.* Colorado Springs: NavPress, 2001.

Collins, Jim. *Good to Great: Why Some Companies Make the Leap...and Others Don't.* New York: Harper Collins, 2001.

Crane, Thomas. *The Heart of Coaching.* San Diego: FTY Press, 1998.

Creswell, Jane. *Christ Centered Coaching: 7 Benefits for Ministry Leaders.* St. Louis: Chalice Press, 2006.

Eblin, Scott. *The Next Level: What Insiders Know About Executive Success.* Palo Alto, Calif.: Davies Black Publishing, 2006.

Engstrom, Ted and Norman Rohrer. *The Fine Art of Mentoring: Passing on to Others What God Has Given to You.* Brentwood, Tenn.: Wolgemuth and Hyatt, 1989.

Fairley, Stephen G. and Chris E. Stout. *Getting Started in Personal and Executive Coaching: How to Create a Thriving Coaching Practice.* Hoboken, N.J.: John C. Wiley & Sons, 2004.

Frazee, Randy. *Making Room for Life: Trading Chaotic Lifestyles for Connected Relationships.* Grand Rapids: Zondervan, 2004.

Gallwey, W. Timothy. *The Inner Game of Tennis.* New York: Random House, 1974.

Gempf, Conrad. *Jesus Asked: What He Wanted to Know.* Grand Rapids: Zondervan, 2003.

Hammett, Edward H., *Spiritual Leadership in a Secular Age.* St. Louis: Lake Hickory Resources, 2005.

Hargrove, Robert. *Masterful Coaching.* San Francisco: Jossey-Bass Pfeiffer, 2003.

Hock, Dee. *Birth of the Chaordic Age.* San Francisco: Berrett-Koehler, 1999.

Hunter, George C., III. *The Celtic Way of Evangelism: How Christianity Can Reach the West...Again.* Nashville: Abingdon Press, 2000.

Hybels, Bill. *Courageous Leadership.* Grand Rapids: Zondervan, 2002.

Kinlaw, Dennis. *Coaching for Commitment.* San Francisco: Jossey-Bass Pfeiffer, 1999.

Lencioni, Patrick. *The Five Dysfunctions of a Team.* San Francisco: Jossey-Bass Pfeiffer, 2002.

Mann, Alan. *Atonement for a "Sinless" Society.* Waynesboro, Ga.: Paternoster, 2005.

O'Neill, Mary Beth. *Executive Coaching with Backbone and Heart: A Systems Approach to Engaging Leaders with Their Challenges.* San Francisco: Jossey-Bass Pfeiffer, 2000.

Peterson, Eugene. *The Contemplative Pastor: Returning to the Art of Spiritual Direction.* Grand Rapids: Eerdmans, 1993.

Whitmore, John. *Coaching for Performance.* London: Nicholas Brealey Publishing Limited, 1992.

Whitworth, Laura, Henry Kimsey-House, and Phil Sandahl. *Co-Active Coaching: New Skills for Coaching People Toward Success in Work and Life.* Palo Alto, Calif.: Davies-Black, 1998.

Training Resources

Christian Coaching Network, www.christiancoaches.com

Christian Track–Institute of Life Coach Training, www.christian-living.com

International Coach Federation, www.coachfederation.org

The Columbia Partnership, www.thecolumbiapartnership.org

Valwood Christian Leadership Coaching, www.valwoodcoaching.org

Western Seminary, www.westernseminary.edu

Other Resources

Allender, Dan. "Mimicking Our Disruptive Father and Our Diverse Older Brother: Learning Prophetic Disruption, Priestly Connection, and Kingly Service." *Mars Hill Review* (Summer 1996): 34–46.

Bullard, George. "Coaching Congregations to Reach Their Full Kingdom Potential." *Net Results* (October 2005): 14–15.

Creswell, Jane. "Stuck Church? What about a Coach?" *Net Results* (Jan 2003): 3–5.

Dempsey, Margaret. "Christian Coaching Transforms Congregations." *Net Results* (March/April 2006): 12.

_____. "Minister/Mother Rediscovers God's Calling." *Net Results* (May/June 2006): 12.

Hall, Chad. "Coaching from the Sideline." *Leadership Journal* (Spring 2005): 62–65.

Hamilton, Kendall. "Need a Life? Get a Coach," *Newsweek* (February 5, 1996): 48.

Miller, Linda. "Counselor or Coach?" *REV Magazine* (September 2003): 54–57.

Net Results magazine has many articles on Christian Coaching; visit www.netresults.org

"The Good to Great Pastor: An Interview with Jim Collins." *Leadership Journal* (Spring 2006): 48–50.

Personality Assessments

Literally hundreds of personality assessments are available. Many for-profit and not-for-profit organizations use these or others that can be incorporated into the coaching conversations.

Myers Briggs

Google: Myers Briggs

http://www.teamtechnology.co.uk/tt/t–articl/mb–simpl.htm

http://www.humanmetrics.com/cgi–win/JTypes1.htm

Myers Briggs presents a model of personality that identifies your personality preferences. This is analogous to handedness. You have two hands. You use them both. But most people are either "right handed" or "left handed." That is, they have a natural inclination or preference for one hand. In a similar way, you have many facets to your personality. You use all of them. However, you have a natural inclination or preference for certain ways of thinking and behaving.

DiSC

Google: DiSC

http://www.resourcesunlimited.com/DiSC_Profiles.asp

http://www.corexcel.com/htmlpersonal.profile.prod.htm?source= adwords&keyword=disc&advert= 397890446

The DiSC Classic Profile is a self-administered, self-scored, personal behavior assessment. Behavioral styles are grouped in four categories, and the participant is guided through an in-depth interpretation of results. The instrument then provides feedback for building on strengths and increasing effectiveness in particular situations. The DiSC Classic Profile enables individuals to:

• Assess personal behavior across four dimensions: dominance, influence, steadiness, and conscientiousness

- Discover their personal behavioral strengths and identify the environment conducive to their success
- Learn about the differences of others and the environment they require for maximum productivity and teamwork

Winslow

Google: Winslow Assessment
http://www.achievementorgroup.com/winslowinfo.html
http://www.thecoachingstaff.com/assessment_technology.htm

The Winslow Personal Assessment and Development Program is designed to give a person a thorough look at his or her complete personality trait structure by using a sophisticated computer behavior assessment program. Twenty-four key personality characteristics are measured to help a person achieve the success and potential he or she is capable of. The Winslow Report includes profile charts, personality traits, influential traits, and personal development. The Winslow Assessment takes into consideration your heredity as well as environment so you can discover the real you. The report shows how to make your weaknesses become your strengths and use your strengths to your advantage for success.

The Columbia
PARTNERSHIP
LEADERSHIP SERIES

Christ-Centered Coaching

7 Benefits for Ministry Leaders

BY JANE CRESWELL

"Coach Jane Creswell is the consummate leader in bringing coaching principles to life in a church or organization. Her words of wisdom will impact your organization more than you can imagine."

■ Laurie Beth Jones, author of *Jesus, CEO; The Path;* and *Jesus, Life Coach*

978-08272-04997

Recreating the Church

Leadership for the Postmodern Age

BY RICHARD L. HAMM

"Dick Hamm asks an essential—and deeply faithful—question of the church: Where are we going? Then, through analysis and insight into both past and future, and with an unwavering commitment to the mission of the church, Hamm points us in the right directions."

■ Wesley Granberg-Michaelson, General Secretary, Reformed Church in America

978-08272-32532

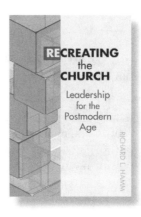

Pursuing the Full Kingdom Potential of Your Congregation

BY GEORGE W. BULLARD JR.

"If you want your church to mature and get beyond the preservation stage and to fulfill God's will for Kingdom growth, then study, read, and pray through this book."

■ Denton Lotz, General Secretary, Baptist World Alliance

978-08272-29846

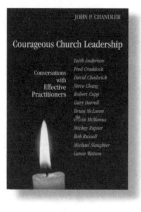

Courageous Church Leadership
Conversations with Effective Practitioners
BY JOHN P. CHANDLER

"Great leadership hinges primarily on one thing—finding the courage to be yourself. Chandler uncovers the stories of some who found that courage and became remarkable leaders."

■ Jim Henderson, executive director of Off-the-Map, former director of leadership development at Vineyard Community Church

978-08272-05062

The Heart of the Matter
Changing the World God's Way
BY CHARLES HALLEY

"With great insight and real world testing, Charlie Halley points out that personal transformation and congregational transformation are inseparable."

■ Don Cousins, congregational coach, former executive director of Willow Creek Community Church

978-08272-14521

Enduring Connections
Creating a Preschool and Children's Ministry
BY JANICE HAYWOOD

Providing a thorough introduction to preschool and children's ministries, Janice Haywood addresses the questions a childhood minister faces and ways to answer them.

978-08272-08216